The Autist's Guide to the Galaxy

The
Autist's
Guide
to the
Galaxy
navigating the world of 'normal people'

Clara Törnvall

Illustrations by Anneli Furmark
Translated from the Swedish by Alice E. Olsson

SCRIBE

Melbourne | London | Minneapolis

Scribe Publications
18–20 Edward St, Brunswick, Victoria 3056, Australia
2 John St, Clerkenwell, London, WC1N 2ES, United Kingdom
3754 Pleasant Ave, Suite 100, Minneapolis, Minnesota 55409, USA

First published as *Vanliga människor: autistens guide till galaxen*
by Natur & Kultur, Sweden 2023
Published by arrangement with Nordin Agency AB, Sweden
First published in English by Scribe 2024

Typeset in Garamond Premier Pro by the publishers

Printed and bound in the UK by CPI Group (UK) Ltd,
Croydon CR0 4YY

Scribe is committed to the sustainable use of natural resources and the
use of paper products made responsibly from those resources.

978 1 761381 02 7 (Australian edition)
978 1 915590 87 9 (UK edition)
978 1 957363 89 9 (US edition)
978 1 761385 81 0 (ebook)

Catalogue records for this book are available from the
National Library of Australia and the British Library.

scribepublications.com.au
scribepublications.co.uk
scribepublications.com

Contents

A note from the author

I am an autist. Autism means thinking, speaking, and moving differently through the world. I don't function the same way as many others. And every day, I put great effort into interpreting people who aren't autistic, adapting to their brains. It's a labour that goes on every waking hour, my whole life.

Most people aren't autists. They are called 'neurotypicals'.

It's hard to know exactly how many neurotypicals there are, since not all neurodivergent people seek a diagnosis. What we do know is that most of the population lacks a neurodevelopmental diagnosis.

This is a book for readers with experience of autism who want to learn to understand 'normal' people better. Their world is strange and puzzling, yet they rarely think of themselves in this way.

In this book, you'll meet autists who share their

experiences of neurotypicals. I'll also include my own tips that might help young autistic readers. These are pieces of advice that have served me well in adulthood, and that I wish I had received sooner. I'm fully aware that all autists are different, and what works for me may not always be right for you. Take what you like and leave the rest.

There are many books about autism written by neurotypicals who want to help autists fit in — that is, behave less autistically. This is not one of those books. This is an autistic guide, written by an autistic guide.

Now let's flip the script.

What it means to be neurotypical

Being neurotypical means that one's brain has developed in a particular way. It means interpreting the world according to certain principles, and thinking, speaking, and moving differently compared to autists.

Since neurotypicals — or NTs as the term is sometimes abbreviated — are in the majority, their way of functioning is thought of as the norm. They are typical. 'Normal' people. The standard model.

Being normal isn't something you can control.

The term 'neurotypical' is neither derogatory nor derisive. It's neutral and often used by neurodivergent people to describe the world around them. It is less commonly used by neurotypicals, as they seldom have to describe themselves. In this book, it simply means a person who is not autistic. (To be more precise, 'allistic' is the correct term for individuals who aren't on the autism spectrum, while 'neurotypical' means not having any neurodevelopmental or psychiatric condition at all. But since the word 'allistic' isn't very established, I will be using the more common term 'neurotypical' throughout this book.)

Being normal isn't something one can control. It has biological causes and does not depend on one's upbringing. If you lack neurodivergence such as autism or ADHD/ADD, it's not due to childhood trauma or how you were raised. Vaccines cannot make you neurotypical. It's a congenital condition.

It's important to understand that being neurotypical is not a mental illness but a way of functioning. It cannot be trained away or resolved through therapy, and there is no medication to cure it.

Neurotypicals often struggle to talk about differences without passing judgement. Many of them believe that being neurotypical is better. Others think that autists who talk about themselves are trying to show off or hold themselves up as superior.

That's not the case, of course. Being autistic is neither better nor worse. It's just as neutral as being neurotypical. Only different.

How to spot a neurotypical

Can you tell if a person is neurotypical simply by looking at them? No, there is no such thing as a specifically neurotypical appearance. They can look like any person. But there are clues to keep an eye out for.

If you spot a person dressed in the latest fashion from a major clothing brand; wearing brand-new, uncomfortable-looking shoes, such as high heels; with lively facial expressions; who regularly exchanges glances with others and appears to feel right at home in a crowd without earplugs or sunglasses — then there is a good chance you have come across a neurotypical.

A society built for the brains of the majority

Our society places high demands on everyone to function the same way. Children are expected to be sufficiently insensitive to sensory stimuli and numb enough to cope with a noisy school environment involving overcrowded classrooms, schedule changes, new teachers, classes being split up, and ever-changing circumstances.

Simply listening to your teacher and studying for your exams by memorising all the details aren't enough. No, as a student you are expected to take responsibility for finding the right facts, delivering engaging oral presentations, leading your own parent–teacher conferences, and analysing your answers at a highly abstract level.

In the West, you are encouraged to become independent early, move out, live alone, and not rely on anyone — not even your family. To achieve this level of independence, you need a job that pays well enough to afford your own place.

In your work life, you need to be resilient enough to endure uncertain conditions and temporary employment. You must be able to accept jobs at short notice, always be flexible, negotiate your salary with polished arguments, be socially competent, engage in small talk in the break room, and thrive as part of a team.

Beyond this, you are expected to have friends as well as multiple hobbies. And a successful love life. You should be able to obtain a driver's license, choose an energy supplier, and pay your bills on time. Learn to walk through revolving doors, book vacations, and scan your items at the self-checkout.

Each person is supposed to be their own multi-competent little universe and manage all aspects of life by themselves. Be good at and know everything.

All this is challenging for anyone to live up to, but for an autist it's all but impossible. This is because the autist functions differently than a neurotypical does. Being autistic in a society built for neurotypicals is like being a square peg trying to fit into a round hole.

All people have strengths and weaknesses. But

they
rarely
think of
themselves
as
strange.

autists have different strengths and weaknesses than neurotypicals. We often find things easy that neurotypicals struggle with, and struggle with things that are easy for them.

The problem is that the norm is based on the majority. If a strange behaviour is found in most of the population, it isn't classified as a disability because almost everyone does it. For this reason, many neurotypicals don't realise that they are the norm. They usually — almost always — assume that everyone functions the same way they do.

Some neurotypicals get annoyed when you tell them you are different. It can be difficult for them to accept that not everyone is the same, and to imagine that there can be different ways of functioning.

If you continue to assert your difference, they may be provoked and think you are bragging or trying to be special. This probably stems from most people wanting to feel unique and be seen for their individual personality. Few like to hear that they are part of the norm. Who wants to feel conventional and be a 'normie'? 'Cis', 'straight', or 'white, middle-aged men' are boring categories to belong to. Not even white middle-aged men want to be white middle-aged men. It sounds so dull.

We live in a culture that claims to celebrate strong individuals who stand apart and go their own way. I'll return to this idea later — and how it isn't always true in practice.

Do I need to add that all people are different and no one — autist or not — can be reduced solely to their way of functioning? If you have met one neurotypical, you have met only one. The same goes for autists. I write this just to be on the safe side, so we have that covered. Now it's time to delve into the often mindboggling world of neurotypicals.

The history of neurotypicals

Throughout human history, normal people have always existed. But we haven't always called them neurotypicals. For a long time, they were simply known as 'people' — while autists have been called everything from holy fools, psychopaths, schizophrenics, handicapped, mentally ill, retarded, oddballs, idiots, eccentrics, and loners, to savants and geniuses.

Neurotypicals have always had opinions about people who function differently than themselves. Often, they have believed *they* know best what an autist needs, despite having no experience of being autistic. This conviction that they are the authority on how to be human is often so deeply ingrained they don't realise when they are being prejudiced.

Prejudice stems from poor mentalisation. Those who express prejudice often lack the will or ability to imagine that someone could feel, think, or experience the world differently than they do.

Throughout history, peer pressure has allowed humanity to build viable communities and cultures. But it has also taken deeply destructive forms, such as groupthink, bullying, war, and terror.

Neurotypicals are often preoccupied with belonging to a group and being part of a context. They are constantly relating to others around them and what these people might think. This makes them less resistant to peer pressure than autists. Neurotypicals like to claim that all people are the same in some fundamental ways, and for this reason they often analyse peer pressure as a force no one can resist.

And indeed, in numerous studies, scientists have demonstrated how difficult it is for the individual to resist the group. One famous example is the psychological experiment conducted in the 1950s by Solomon Asch. In groups where participants were asked to assess the length of different lines, all test subjects except one were instructed to give the wrong answer. Despite the others being obviously incorrect, the lone participant didn't dare to trust their own judgement and go against the group — and ended up giving the wrong answer too.

Many years later, in 2014, a similar experiment was conducted — this time with autistic and neurotypical children. It turned out that the autistic children more often gave the correct answer and pointed out the line of the right length. They trusted themselves and resisted peer pressure.

And yet, the conclusion of most peer pressure research has been that all people are equally susceptible to it. Everyone is at risk of being affected, neurotypicals like to claim. The problem is that this isn't true. Everyone isn't affected, even though the majority is. While most people fall in line, a few have the courage not to. History is full of individuals who resisted and went their own way, even when the price for doing so was high.

As long as neurotypicals pretend that no one can assert their independence against a united group, we won't learn enough about either personal morals or collective destructive forces. From this perspective, acquiescence seems inevitable. It would be better if research focused on the outliers. Why don't they toe the line, when that's the easiest option? What gives them the courage to challenge the majority?

Autistic voices

Choli: 'When you ask a neurotypical to explain what they mean, they just repeat themselves, more slowly. It's like, I heard you the first time — but that doesn't mean I get it.'

Fabian: 'If I tell them it doesn't work that way for me, they'll just say, "Then make it work." I don't want their pity. I just wish they'd be a little more considerate.'

Bea: 'I had this close friend who was staying with me since she was new in town and didn't have her own place yet. I was going through a bit of rough patch with my boyfriend and asked her to go and stay somewhere else over the weekend, to give us some alone time. But after the weekend she didn't come back, and I asked what had happened. "You kicked me out, so I'm staying in a hotel," she told me. When all I'd said was give me the weekend, she had taken it to mean something else. But I hadn't wanted her to move out.

There were lots of misunderstandings like that, when she'd bottle up her anger and explode years later. I was completely distraught. Turns out, she'd been reading all sorts of things into my words and actions, when really I meant exactly what I said and did. The whole thing was exhausting, and it took me years to recover from the hurt and overcome my fear of making friends again.'

How neurotypicals experience the world

For autists, the boundaries between humans, animals, nature, and objects can blur, and words can mean almost anything. Neurotypicals don't have the same fluid approach. Their perception — that is, the way they process their surroundings — works differently. It's as if neurotypicals have an automatic camera with certain pre-sets to help them interpret the world around them. When reading their surroundings, they place what they see, hear, and feel into pre-existing categories. Since their sensory impressions can be sorted under ready-made labels, they can quickly form an image.

When autists experience the world, we aren't quite as automated. Our camera is manual. Before we snap a picture, we must first adjust the focus and shutter speed and find the right light. It's time-consuming and requires a lot of preparation. For us, each situation is unique. We start from scratch every time, noticing a detail and piecing it together with other details until a picture emerges. It costs us a lot of energy.

Humans interpret the world through cultural patterns and codes. In his book *A Field Guide to Earthlings: an autistic/Asperger view of neurotypical behaviour*, American author Ian (now Star) Ford describes how we experience reality through a web of symbols linked together by associations. Such mental connections can arise between: words that sound alike such as 'cat' and 'hat'; pieces of knowledge acquired at the same time in life; words with similar meanings; and symbols associated with something important to you, or that share the same context.

People with similar symbolic webs belong to a shared culture. Individuals who have lived in the same environment for a long time develop similar associations between symbols. Yet each individual makes the associations on their own and connects the meaning with things they already know, which is why symbols can be interpreted differently.

A newborn baby has no filter against the outside world, so its parents make sure to protect the child from loud noises, bright light, and emotional outbursts. Over time, the child will gradually become desensitised and develop a filter to block out stimuli. If the child is neurotypical, that is.

As an adult autist, it can feel like the child's view of the world never truly left you. The world appears unpredictable, fluid, and enchanted. Your associations follow other patterns. Thursday, 8.00 pm, and the colour green are the same, yet you struggle to explain why. They just are. A factory chimney and an umbilical cord are also linked. So are a black crystal and the dark screen of a TV.

When the neurotypical infant in the example above grows older, its eyes and ears will still see and hear with the same acuity, but its brain will process the stimuli differently. Impressions will no longer enter unfiltered and with full force. Instead, the brain sorts through and forwards the incoming signals. It converts stimuli into a symbolic representation of reality. The real world is transformed into words and made less complex. In the brain, a behemoth of glass, concrete, steel beams, and thousands of different parts becomes simply a 'house'.

In other words, language is a simplification and reduction of data. The neurotypical brain is good at filtering. Its web of symbols forms templates or stencils of reality. The stencils are used as filters to identify objects and phenomena and quickly make the right connections. For this to work, the stencils must consist of a kind of minimal symbolic, cultural essence — the detail without which the thing doesn't exist.

Put more simply: A hare needs its long ears not to be a rabbit, an alpaca its fluffy hairdo not to be a llama, a toad its pocked skin not to be a frog.

Or take the sea lion: without its ears and powerful front flippers, it could easily be mistaken for a seal. But if these two unique features are present, it's just as easy to identify a sea lion in a hastily drawn sketch as in a detailed photograph of the animal. As long as the few pencil strokes are sufficiently meaningful, a sea lion stencil arises.

When the neurotypical brain quickly sorts information into categories, it only processes the data that fits the stencil. It registers 'ears + large front flippers' and quickly concludes: a sea lion. The rest — the irrelevant details — it filters out.

That's not how an autistic brain works. It processes all the details and doesn't filter out those that are unimportant.

When humans communicate, we use words, gestures, symbols, facial expressions, sounds, and body

SEAL

SEALION

language. Communication happens on many levels simultaneously. We also communicate through things such as clothes, events, sports, cultural expression, and architecture, as well as through our religious and political views.

When neurotypicals perceive the world, they can register a multitude of stimuli — all at the same time. Let's say they are taking part in a conversation. While hearing the words being spoken, they process their meaning. Simultaneously, they can sense the intention and the hidden messages behind the words, read their conversation partner's facial expressions, and notice other things happening in the room.

This seems like an almost staggering capacity for multitasking. Yet the reason they can do so many things at once is, as we have seen, that their brains filter out details deemed irrelevant in the moment. Neurotypicals process symbols and categories, not all the details that make up the whole.

This multitasking superpower depends on the context being reasonably familiar. Should they find themselves in a foreign culture, however, the process of decoding isn't quite as straightforward. Then it requires more effort.

It is often said that people communicate primarily

through non-verbal cues — that is, gestures, tone, and different ways of showing how they feel with their bodies. Neurotypicals do this more and in a different way than autists do. Their non-verbal communication is social. They often use facial expressions and body language to broadcast their place within a group. In conversation, they mix verbal and unspoken messages effortlessly and trust that they will be understood.

Autists tend to focus more on the words — what is said and written. This doesn't mean that we never pick up on silent cues or body language. We can find ourselves in a room where the air is thick with subtext and notice that hidden messages are being circulated without understanding what they are. It's confusing when what we feel doesn't match the words being spoken.

Let's say I meet someone who asks how I'm doing. The question signals an interest in me and my wellbeing. Yet at the same time, I can sense with my body that the other person isn't interested in truly knowing how I am, or is too stressed and doesn't have the time or presence of mind to listen and process my answer. The mismatch between the words and the silent signals makes the situation frustrating.

When neurotypicals communicate verbally, they

often assume that the words mean something more than they actually do. For them, the literal meaning — the one(s) listed in the dictionary — is merely one part of the word's whole, expanded significance.

This makes dealing with neurotypicals tricky. They couch their words in a shroud of secret, additional meanings. Deciphering this fluff requires a lot of energy, and they may not be willing to tell you outright what they mean.

Sometimes, a direct question scares them, and they take offence. This is because they assume that you function like they do and have already understood the underlying message. And still, you ask. Why? They get suspicious. You must be implying something else; surely, the question can't be sincere. What do you really mean? Are you trying to catch them out? Or get the upper hand? Thus, they obsess.

Things neurotypicals say and how you can respond

'**Everyone is neurodivergent these days.**' No. Most people don't have a neurodevelopmental diagnosis.

'**Isn't everyone a little autistic?**' No. That's like saying everyone is a little allergic just because they have sneezed once or twice. Or that butter is a bit like cake just because it's a common ingredient *in* cake. People who say this often believe that autism simply means being introverted and not always coping with everyday life. But autism is much more complex and multifaceted.

'**Don't make autism your identity.**' Why not? You only say that because you think of autism as something bad. Autism means I function unlike you in many ways. My brain is wired differently. Why wouldn't it be my identity? It's not my whole identity, but it's an important part of it.

'Have you tried exercising?' Physical activity improves our wellbeing and can alleviate anxiety and mild to moderate depression, but it doesn't make you less autistic.

'Have you tried using a calendar to get more organised?' I truly wish it were that simple. If I could plan, make schedules, and use a calendar, of course I would.

'Go outside and get some fresh air, it'll make you feel better!' No, I feel just as good indoors, and even better when I get to focus on my special interest.

'You're exaggerating, it's not that bad.' You couldn't possibly know, since you lack the experience. Some days are harder than others.

'Everyone struggles with that.' No. Everyone goes through sorrow and uncertainty, and many people suffer, but only autists struggle with being autistic in a world built for neurotypicals.

'You can't possibly be autistic because you: have a sense of humour/don't look autistic/meet my gaze/ are empathetic/have a good job/aren't at all like my cousin's autistic child who throws themselves on the floor screaming.' You can't possibly be neurotypical, because you just made an independent decision without anxiously checking what everyone around you thinks/ wear comfortable shoes/say what you think/have a special interest that's important to you/remove the laundry tags from your clothes.

'Don't call yourself disabled.' Why not? I am. Not because there is something wrong with me, but because society isn't designed to accommodate all ways of functioning. If society changed, I would no longer be disabled. Yet I would still be autistic.

People can call themselves whatever they want. The autist's difficulties remain, regardless of what they are called or how you think about them.

'Too many people are diagnosed with autism these days.' I think you feel that way because autism has begun to be named and identified, which wasn't the case in the past. Yet autism is a human condition that has always existed. Being diagnosed doesn't make us autistic; we already were. Just like gravity didn't suddenly arise when Newton discovered it in the late 1600s. A diagnosis is a confirmation — it doesn't create anything.

Autistic people need to know they are autistic; otherwise, they can't help themselves to a better life. Autists shouldn't have to suffer just because some neurotypicals think society 'should' be free of diagnoses.

'No one's normal.' Sure, that sounds nice, and I get that you don't want to be lame and normative. Of course, it's just as 'normal', in the sense of 'natural', to be autistic as not to be.

But norms and normality do exist, in the sense of 'the majority' and 'most people'. Claiming otherwise is nothing but denial and wishful thinking. The norm is often referred to using the shorthand 'we'. But autists (and other minorities) are rarely included in that collective.

'There's no such thing as autistic culture.' Actually, there is. Autists are different in similar ways. We experience the world differently, which affects our verbal and artistic expression. Since words and their worlds lie wide-open before our eyes and are reconquered each day, our pursuit of the hidden meaning of words can inspire an original use of language with new associations and analogies. This can be challenging for neurotypicals to pick up on. But autists recognise each other in an instant.

'You appear to struggle more with autism since you got your diagnosis. You seemed to be doing better before?' I wasn't. I struggled a lot, you just didn't see it. When I found out that I am autistic, I understood my difficulties better and I no longer try to hide them.

Three ways of interpreting difference

When neurotypicals encounter people who function differently, their reactions and attitudes can vary. Often, they view difference in one of the following ways:

1. **Self-inflicted/imagined.** The difference is seen as a defect that the person in question consciously creates and therefore deserves. These people think the difference could go away if the other person were willing to make an effort: 'They say they're autistic, but they should just try harder.'

2. **Medical.** The difference is seen as a defect, but one that the other person didn't create and has no power over. Something is 'broken' inside the autist, who isn't to blame for it and can't fix themselves. Either the difference is viewed as permanent, or

these people think it can be remedied with the help of medical expertise: 'They *suffer* from autism.'

3. **One way of functioning among several.** The difference is viewed as neutral — neither a defect nor a superpower: 'They can't peel an orange/don't like changing plans/communicate literally, etc.'

When a person is diagnosed with autism, they fall into the second category: the medical view. In this category, you are more shielded from bullying and prejudice since neurotypicals don't consider it to be the autist's own fault. Bullying someone for a defect they can't control is crude and tasteless, they argue.

Yet, in this category you are also more easily belittled and stigmatised. A diagnosis turns you into a helpless patient who doesn't know what's best for yourself. Someone to pity, whose voice doesn't count.

When the difference is viewed as self-inflicted, people are free to pass judgement. This is why neurotypicals can say things like 'I don't think they're *really* autistic'. By removing the neurodevelopmental condition entirely, they can put the autistic person back into the 'get your act together' category and thus judge and bully them without feeling guilty.

Many neurotypicals either feel sorry for or are provoked by people whose brains are different than theirs. Difference can only evoke their sympathy or aggression. They often struggle to see it for what it is: simply a variation, neither better nor worse.

Not everyone is like this, of course. But enough for autists to be met with prejudice.

Understanding others

In a scientific experiment, two audiences — one autistic and one neurotypical — were shown selected scenes from *Who's Afraid of Virginia Woolf?* The film, starring Elizabeth Taylor and Richard Burton, portrays a married couple whose facade cracks during a dinner party, revealing old conflicts and wounds.

The purpose of the experiment was to study how autists interpret social interaction. As it turned out, the autists and neurotypicals directed their gaze at different things. While the autists focused on the actors' mouths and the words coming out of them, the neurotypicals concentrated on the actors' eyes.

The neurotypicals invested their energy in interpreting everything the actors *didn't* say — the silences, the subtext, stolen glances, or the facial expressions of a supporting character in the background. For this reason, they could recall very little of what had been said, whereas the autists remembered the words and could recite long passages of dialogue.

When the findings were presented, the neurotypical researchers emphasised the difficulties autists faced in picking up on unspoken messages, but said nothing about their powerful and accurate memories.

Yet who struggles more — a person who forgets what's been said, or someone who's missed what wasn't said? Couldn't what's viewed as the autist's limitation also count as an advantage? Here, the majority has decided the neurotypical way is the right and most desirable one. The other way — that of the autist — is classed as aberrant and inferior.

Are they listening to what we say? Or are they absorbed by their own interpretation? These are questions you might ask yourself when interacting with neurotypicals.

The answer is probably that they often interpret more than they listen.

In the 1950s, a study was conducted on how people extract meaning from conversations. The researcher, Albert Mehrabian, concluded that only 7 per cent of people receiving a spoken message focused mostly on the words being said. Meanwhile, 38 per cent focused mostly on the tone of voice, and 55 per cent — the largest group — attached greatest importance to the speaker's body language.

Presumably, the autists belonged to the 7 per cent.

Since neurotypicals are so preoccupied with non-verbal social communication, they often want to see with their own eyes that you are listening to them. They like it when you show with your body that you are paying attention. You may need to lean forward, nod, and look them in the eyes to truly convince them.

If you are doodling or taking notes while they talk, they may think you aren't hearing what they are saying. They can't always grasp that this is simply a way of processing stimuli. They might mistake it for a sign of concentration issues, since you don't 'look' attentive.

Simply conveying information and cutting straight to the point is often quicker than other forms of communication. For this reason, neurotypicals can come across as digressive and long-winded. Communicating vaguely and non-verbally is more time-consuming, and neurotypicals sometimes need to fill this time with words. This is why they can be known to repeat themselves and say things that are void of meaning.

You often hear this when people communicate in a professional role. They add in filler phrases such as 'in the situation in which we find ourselves right now'.

Neurotypical speech can contain so many contradictions and strange insinuations that the main message is incomprehensible. Sometimes, the content seems so watered down that it's about everything and nothing at the same time. *What is this person trying to say?* the autist might think to themselves impatiently. In these cases, you need to remember that NTs don't always communicate primarily to convey information. Sometimes they talk to create associations between positive values, show support for others, evoke a sense of solidarity and belonging, or point out a common goal. Some people talk just to feel that they exist.

Much NT communication is about trying to exert influence. They want to manipulate others or their own status within a certain group. This can be why they repeat the same message so many times. They are trying to persuade you. They think you mean something other than what you said, and that you might change your mind the next time you hear the same words. For an autist — who remembers everything that's been said — it can be exhausting to have to hear these repetitions.

Hello! On greetings

Many neurotypicals like to touch when they greet, even when meeting people they don't know. They want to shake hands, hug, or kiss each other on the cheek. Since they aren't hypersensitive to sensory stimuli, they don't experience touch as unpleasant or overly intimate. It doesn't make their skin crawl or cause them physical pain.

Shaking hands is important to them, and they assign great significance to how firm or weak your handshake is. If you want to please them, your handshake should be moderately firm. Too weak, and it'll be perceived as limp and impolite. Yet if you squeeze too tightly, they'll think you are trying to assert your power and superiority.

They also find it strange when a handshake lasts too long. In *Comedians Without Borders*, a Swedish TV show in which participants are tasked with doing embarrassing things in public while being filmed with hidden cameras, one of the challenges is to shake hands with a stranger for as long as possible. The unspoken social rule for handshakes is that they should last between one and three seconds, the host explains. The seconds tick by and the audience shrieks with equal parts terror and delight as participants maintain their grip for as long as possible.

A greeting ritual is important for neurotypicals — even when they meet close friends or relatives with whom they socialise on a regular basis. They are reluctant to skip it. The greeting becomes a validation of being seen by the person they greet.

For autists, greetings may seem unnecessary when meeting people we already know. When my autistic friend Hanna and I meet, we nod at each other, smile, and say a quick hello. Then we promptly dive into a conversation about whatever is on our minds. We don't need to hug, for we already know that we like the other person and enjoy each other's company.

Neurotypicals prefer a uniform way of greeting. Ideally, everyone should do the same. If they encounter someone who doesn't greet them the right way, they can feel provoked. Refusing to shake someone's hand is quite rude, of course, but neurotypicals may perceive it as being on par with denying the other person's existence.

This tradition is rooted, in part, in the historical use of a handshake to seal a promise. When striking a business agreement, you shake hands. The handshake is a sign of honour, and to grasp someone's hand is to show them respect. Not accepting an extended hand is therefore a powerful gesture that signals unreliability.

Where I live, in Sweden, hugging has become increasingly popular. But during the Covid-19 pandemic, when handshakes and hugs were no longer possible, new ways of greeting through touch were invented. People bumped elbows, or stood on one leg and rubbed their feet together. You could also embrace yourself and extend your arms to demonstrate that you would have liked to hug the other person.

The pandemic also led to a temporary reassessment of the handshake. If the act of touching could lead to a dangerous illness, it was no longer as important. Recommendations *not* to shake hands were introduced to prevent the spread of infection. Yet just a few years earlier, in countries such as France and Switzerland, Muslims had been denied citizenship after refusing to shake hands with officials of the opposite sex.

NTs also like you to look them in the eyes when greeting and speaking to them. At the same time, they don't want you to stare. This can be tricky to navigate. If you don't look them in the eyes during a conversation, they think you aren't listening to what they are saying and feel hurt. If your gaze happens to linger for too long, they might get offended and ask what you are 'staring at'.

The group rules

As we have seen, many neurotypicals relate their sense of self to a group around them. It's as if they define themselves in relation to an invisible collective. They carry this network of relationships in their mind as they move through life and make decisions.

For them, having many friends is typically an indicator of high status. The more friends they have, the more liked they feel. The group's approval is important for their wellbeing.

Some neurotypicals engage in almost compulsive socialising, both over the phone and face to face. They spend all their time maintaining social contacts and seeing friends, which can lead them to neglect other aspects of life. For example, they may struggle to develop true special interests. They simply don't have the time.

Since neurotypicals often identify themselves in

relation to a group, their opinions can come to depend on what others think.

Suppose that a neurotypical is planning a trip to London and wants to visit the Madame Tussauds wax museum. They mention it to a friend, who responds: 'Only stupid tourists go there.' Since the neurotypical doesn't want to be perceived as a 'stupid tourist', they change their mind and no longer want to visit the museum. Being part of the right group is more important than their personal desires.

Of course, autists can behave this way too, but the drive is stronger in neurotypicals. They carry their invisible network in their mind wherever they go.

Neurotypicals often struggle to interpret and understand autists' intentions. They are so used to being the norm that they assume everyone else functions the same way they do. This assumption is often correct — since their way of functioning is that of the majority — but when they encounter an autist, things can go awry.

Autists may struggle to understand neurotypicals, but since we encounter people who function differently than us all the time, we become trained — and often proficient — in dealing with the unfamiliar in others.

Nor do we struggle to understand other autists.

One downside of the neurotypical way of functioning is that they can be quick to judge. Since they base their interpretations on what they already know, they can be sloppy. They don't see each situation separately. Instead, they jump to quick, incorrect conclusions.

When neurotypicals interpret other people's behaviour, they often assume that the intention can be deciphered from the action. They think they can figure out *why* a person behaved a certain way simply by looking at *what* they did. They can't be certain, of course, yet they apply their preconceived notion that all people are the same.

Those who base their conclusions on what they already know also tend to think inside the box. It's difficult for them to think in new ways and imagine something they don't already know or have experience of.

Another downside is that neurotypicals often assume the worst. They can be suspicious and think that others have selfish motives and want to hurt them.

This is a matter of subtext. In every conversation, text message, or communication of any kind, neurotypicals expect there to be a hidden meaning — something that isn't said but which the person communicating nevertheless means. Neurotypicals try to decipher this unspoken message by studying your body language and facial expressions, listening to your tone of voice, or analysing what you have written.

Constantly assuming that no one actually means what they say — isn't that an onerous way to live? Doesn't it make it worse if you also assume that others are hiding things out of spite and malice?

Neurotypicals can be provoked if, as an autist, you ask them a lot of questions. This is because they see the questions as an attempt to challenge or criticise them. But when an autistic person asks 'Why?', they are usually expressing a genuine desire to understand the neurotypical. It's not an attempt to belittle or corner them.

We ask because we are curious and want to know, nothing else. There is no malicious subtext, sarcasm, or passive aggression. We mean what we say and say what we mean. On the Swedish version of the TV show *Married at First Sight*, where participants seeking love are paired off by experts, one of the female participants had survived a brain tumour. After she told her new husband about this experience, the show's psychologists analysed the conversation. In a studio discussion, they talked about how to respond when a person shares something with you in confidence. What should you say when someone tells you about a difficult experience?

Referring to yourself and sharing a difficult experience of your own is a 'cardinal error', the experts agreed. You shouldn't do it too soon, or the other person will feel like you 'stole the conversation' and 'didn't read' their needs. It won't be received as though you are doing it to make the other person feel less alone in their experience.

The experts assumed that the conversation partner sharing their own trauma wants to elevate themselves and be the centre of attention — that the motive is selfish.

Being suspicious of others' motives and interpreting them as signs of self-centeredness is very neurotypical. Autists often speak without constantly calibrating the power dynamics in the conversation. We don't keep track of status and who is superior or inferior. We present interesting problems or examples to each other, without judgement.

But neurotypicals often expect their conversation partners to have an ulterior motive. You could even say they are looking for signs that they aren't being seen because that's their greatest fear. How afraid a neurotypical is varies depending on their self-esteem, of course. But generally, they struggle to understand that

Autistic voices

Rebecca: 'I often find that NTs have less imagination than autists, even though many say the opposite. They always assume that everyone is the same — and that everyone is like them.'

Ellinor: 'They like to whine about things and dwell on problems but don't want solutions. If you offer constructive suggestions, there's no response. Instead, you have to listen to the same story all over again.'

Lina: 'When you talk about a subject, they often think you're actually talking about yourself. They assume you're being manipulative or pushing some hidden agenda.'

Thina: 'I say what I mean and mean what I say. The thing about neurotypicals is that they insist on "reading between the lines" and claiming that I meant something totally different. But if they choose to hear a bunch of weird stuff, that's on them — I don't work that way.'

Ella: 'Sometimes when I don't want to disappoint them, I desperately try to come up with some "hidden meaning" to share. But then I realise … there just isn't one.'

Casper: 'You ever notice how, in a discussion, they rarely stick to the subject? Like, you ask a question about the law and they're off on some tangent about their personal opinions. But that isn't relevant to what's legal and what's not.'

Sofia: 'Many, especially healthcare professionals, ask such open-ended questions that I find it hard to understand what they want to know. "How do you feel about everything?" and "What do you think about what I've just told you?" It's all so broad that I don't know how to respond. I appreciate more specific questions, like: "How are your studies going?" Otherwise, I don't understand what they want to know; surely they're not interested in a detailed account of everything that's going on in my life?'

Fanny: 'They expect you to be a mind reader.'

Mynta: 'They always have to be so indirect and turn everything into a social game, instead of being straightforward and to the point. It seems so complicated and silly.'

Erika: 'They'll bring up a topic but then they don't really want to talk about it. They're just skimming the surface of everything. And if I get interested and want to delve deeper, they act like *I'm* strange. It makes it so clear that they're just talking to exchange sounds, not information.'

Sofia: 'In a discussion, they always have to repeat what you're saying to show they're on the same page. I suppose that can be useful in situations of conflict — to show that you're not *just* disagreeing. But if we're brainstorming, I'd rather move the thought process forward than keep parroting each other.'

Misunderstandings

Neurotypicals struggle with judgement-free, literal communication. They tend to read something more into what you are saying. They draw conclusions based on their own cultural patterns and stencils, rather than on what is actually being said. When you are speaking to them, they receive a multitude of messages simultaneously — not just the words being spoken but also the 'fluff' around the words, all of which they evaluate in an instant and place into pre-existing categories. The problem is that they can jump to the wrong conclusions.

For example, imagine that you are talking to someone who likes the Linux operating system. You might say: 'The Linux logo is a penguin. I don't like penguins.' If you are speaking to a neurotypical, they will likely interpret you as saying that you don't like Linux — even though that wasn't at all what you said. These were two independent statements, yet the neurotypical linked them together. The association between Linux and the penguin meant that they melded into one in the neurotypical's mind. At the same time, they registered your non-verbal cues, perhaps reacting to your neutral expression or lack of eye contact. Based on this, they concluded that you 'seemed displeased', which reinforced the idea that what you actually wanted to say was that Linux is bad.

This is how misunderstandings arise. Some neurotypicals are so set in their categories and past experiences that they can't absorb new information that contradicts their existing belief system. Instead, they hear what they want to hear.

When it comes to perception and cognition, neurotypicals take shortcuts and can, therefore, make quicker connections. They reduce details into symbols and categories; they turn the trees into a forest.

But those who take shortcuts are also quick to generalise.

Let's take an example: NTs have learned that if a person is looking down, it often means they are sad. So, when they encounter someone gazing down, they conclude that this person must be feeling low — even though there are a multitude of reasons that someone might cast their eyes down.

This is the background to the enduring prejudice that autistic people lack empathy. NT doctors and researchers have misinterpreted autists' non-verbal cues — such as a neutral facial expression — and read them as signs of indifference. Then, in the name of science, they have taken the liberty of describing people with a different way of functioning than their own as inferior. Early autism researchers who believed that autists felt no empathy simply lacked imagination when encountering someone unlike themselves.

Today, we know that autistic individuals are often hyper-empathetic and have no trouble feeling compassion. On the contrary, we often display strong civil courage, and the ability to speak out against injustice as we are able to resist peer pressure.

Due to our difficulty detecting lies, however, autists are more often victimised. Research shows that autists are at a higher risk of being subjected to sexual abuse, as we are easy prey for perpetrators. Autists interpret communication literally and trust that others mean what they say. We may also struggle to listen to our gut, since we are often told that what we feel isn't accurate.

But the prejudice about our supposed inability to feel empathy persists. Just peek at any of the true crime threads on Reddit, and you'll find amateur detectives claiming that the culprit is likely autistic because they 'have no empathy'. In reality, empathy deficits are more common in narcissists and individuals with antisocial personality disorder. Not in autists.

My day job is to produce radio shows about music. One time at work, I pointed out that a program that was supposed to feature calm music didn't. I thought it was a neutral observation: the music was lively and dramatic, not calm and relaxing. I wasn't trying to criticise anyone. But it was received as if I meant something like: 'Why can't you people choose the right music for once?' Most likely, I hadn't couched the message correctly.

If an autistic person doesn't adapt to the neurotypical way of communicating, it doesn't matter if the information itself is factually correct. It may be entirely accurate, yet the message risks being received negatively.

In any given communication, a neurotypical tends to first hear the content they associate with a value judgement and with their position within the group's hierarchy. Not until the next step do they perceive the factual content. And if the recipient hears only threats to their identity, they won't be receptive to the actual, literal message at all. Conflict may arise if the neurotypical reads criticism into the message, whether it's there or not.

For instance, they may suspect autists of trying to please or placate others, when — in fact — we are simply asserting our own independent stance. Neurotypicals are often geared towards competition and rivalry in their social interactions, so they are looking for evidence of it in others.

This can be tricky to rectify. I sometimes apologise in advance — 'I'm autistic, so I'm sorry if I sound blunt' — before saying exactly what I want and mean. There is no point in trying to sugar-coat the message — I don't know how to, and neurotypicals are so unpredictable in what offends them.

Yet constantly having to apologise isn't sustainable for one's self-esteem. Unfortunately, it's a habit many autists develop to avoid rubbing someone the wrong way. It can also make us a little paranoid. When experience has taught us that we will inevitably hurt someone, we become overly vigilant and fear that we are doing it all the time.

Most autists have memories of upsetting others without understanding why. They've received more than their fair share of scolding and surliness; perhaps they have been teased, rejected, used, and discarded. It's not so strange for them to worry it will happen again and to grow cautious.

Here, it would be helpful if neurotypicals could learn not to always assume the worst.

There is an old Swedish proverb that goes: 'As you know thyself, so you know others.' This aptly describes the way neurotypicals interpret others as if they have hidden, selfish motives. This can take many forms. For instance, they may think that you 'shouldn't' post messages of mourning on social media when someone famous has died — they see this as a way of associating yourself with a celebrity in order to appear special. 'Speak for yourself,' I want to respond.

The idea that one's motive could be admiration for the deceased because they have made music or written books that meant a lot in one's own life doesn't seem to cross their minds. As you know thyself, you also know others.

Neurotypicals can also be suspicious of other people's self-descriptions and accuse them of being fake or bragging. 'Those who claim to be thinking about the Roman Empire are lying. The latest trend is just a new way of saying, "I'm highly intellectual and deep",' read a recent editorial published in the Swedish newspaper *Dagens Nyheter*.

Bullies operate in a similar way. They attribute negative qualities to their victim, constructing rules that they claim the victim has broken, making it okay for the bully to judge them. That way, it's the victim's own fault.

Both children and adults bully others. Bullies choose their victims and opportunities; they know what they are doing and count on not getting caught.

Communicating clearly is a challenge for many neurotypicals. The norm is to express yourself in an indirect and vague manner. Neurotypicals only use precision and exactitude in the world of law. In most other contexts, they assume that everyone understands their coded language.

The autist **Henrik** remembers a situation when he was picking up a TV in a rehearsal space he had rented together with a few others. Their lease had been terminated, and the space had to be emptied. One of the landlords wrote to him: 'Don't forget to drop off the keys and the fob while you're there.'

'When I picked up the TV, I reflected on not being able to lock up as I left. But I had been instructed to leave the keys, so I did.

'After I left, I wrote to the landlord that I had returned the keys and the fob and left them inside. He got very upset that I hadn't locked the door behind me. But he'd told me to leave the keys? Apparently, he meant that there was a reception desk in the building where I should have dropped off the keys, but he'd never mentioned that. No one had told me about any such place.'

Not only did the landlord give unclear instructions, but he also responded angrily that Henrik should have used his 'common sense', and blamed and shamed Henrik for making him 'go in on his day off' to solve the problem.

This situation is an example of how neurotypicals can struggle to give clear instructions because they assume that things are obvious. They also have difficulty grasping that autists can do exactly as they are told without meaning to cause trouble for anyone else.

BUT... WHAT'S GOING ON?

NOTHING.

With neurotypicals, there are a million pitfalls you may accidentally stumble into during conversations, both in writing and in speech. It can feel as though you have to carefully weigh each word. Some situations are a balancing act where you simply can't get it right. This, you just have to accept.

Particularly sensitive situations can arise if you, for example, ask someone whether they want children. It's assumed that you are looking to force them into some nuclear family norm, or you risk triggering their grief over failed attempts to get pregnant.

It can also be perceived as insensitive to ask someone how they pronounce their name, where they are from, or what their future plans are. I don't mean that you shouldn't ask. On the contrary, I think many neurotypicals need to get better at not interpreting sincere questions as an attack on their person.

Autistic voices

Liv: 'When I was six or seven, I had a hard time navigating the way my teachers would tell us we must never be mean or use violence — yet at the same time, they'd excuse certain students (especially the boys) when they behaved like bullies or were violent. The teachers always said, "If someone is being mean, tell a grown-up." But when I did, it wasn't uncommon for the grown-up to say, "Ignore them, and they'll stop." Meanwhile, they said nothing to the bully.'

Eva: 'In the autumn of 2017, I made my teacher colleagues roar with laughter when one of them excitedly announced, "The Rolling Stones are coming here in October." I thought, "What on earth — they're coming here, to the school?" and expressed my surprise.'

Sara: 'I went to see a doctor who asked all these questions about my lifestyle. At one point he asked, "How much do you drink?" I said, "Two litres a day." The doctor and his assistant looked puzzled. Then he said, "*What* do you drink?" And I replied, "Lemon water and soy milk."'

Fabian was six years old when he was diagnosed with autism. He was bullied at school, especially in lower secondary school.

'They didn't beat me up or anything, but they would say things. There was this girl I liked. She even suggested we meet up. But right before, I get a call saying she's cancelling. It turned out she had a boyfriend. I think she was making a fool out of me.

'Another time, some eighth graders threw firecrackers at me. I got scared and told my parents. Another time, I saw weird posts about me on my Facebook feed. I guess you could call me naïve but ... I thought they were just messing around. When I showed my parents, they said, "You need to change schools." My mum wrote on my profile, "Why are you doing this to the sweetest kid in the world?" The next day, she told my teacher I wouldn't be coming back.'

Klara: 'I get the feeling that NT people's special interest is other people's lives. I just don't get how they can be so insanely interested in other people's children, grandchildren, partners, relationships, and stuff. Like, on Fridays they can spend the whole day quizzing everyone about their weekend plans, with a million follow-up questions. And then there's people who learn the names of everyone's siblings and grandchildren, and want to talk about their confirmations, graduations, weddings, divorces, even their toddlers' ear infections.'

Anna: 'I genuinely don't care about other people's lives. Like when I'm at someone's house and they want to give me a tour. Apparently, this is a thing people do. So I wander around politely, saying "ahh" and "ooh" and "so nice" whenever it seems appropriate. But, really, I'm just not that interested.

'Don't get me wrong — I care about my friends, but not their interior design preferences or who they're dating. I'm interested in their thoughts and opinions, their passions, their take on the world, not just surface matters.'

Malin: 'Whenever my boyfriend and I were out boating, he had this habit of announcing, "We're coming up to the pier." I thought it was strange that he said it every time. And without fail, it was always followed by him half-yelling, "For the love of god, fend us off!" I remember thinking, "Must he always sound so angry when he asks?" This was before we suspected I was autistic. When he said, "Now we're coming up to the pier," what he really meant was, "Please get ready to fend us off."'

Lina: 'I used to be in a long-distance relationship. He'd drive six hours from his place to mine every other weekend. Each time, I'd ask if he wanted me to make dinner in time for when he'd arrive. Each time, he'd say it wasn't necessary. Each time, he'd also call when he was ten miles away to report that he was at a certain rest stop taking a break. I never understood why he called to say that, and he never understood why I didn't have dinner ready when he got here.'

Hedvig: 'Last summer, I went to visit my grandmother. It was a chilly summer's day, which I found quite pleasant since I tend to run hot. The door to the patio was open and I was out there, probably fussing over

66

some plants, when Grandma popped her head out to ask if I wasn't cold. "No," I replied cheerfully, "it's nice and cool." "Are you sure?" — "Oh yes."

'But a few minutes later, she came and asked the same question again. I assured her that I wasn't cold, and Grandma went inside once more. I noticed that she sounded a bit disappointed, though. So I got up, went into the kitchen and said, "You know, if you're feeling chilly and want to close the door, that's fine too." And wouldn't you know, that's exactly what she wanted.'

Small talk

One of the things Ford Prefect had always found hardest to understand about humans was their habit of continually stating and repeating the very very obvious, as in It's a nice day, *or* You're very tall, *or* Oh dear you seem to have fallen down a thirty-foot well, are you all right?

Douglas Adams, *The Hitchhiker's Guide to the Galaxy*

Neurotypicals like to talk even when they don't really have anything to say, and it doesn't much matter what they are talking about. For them, social interaction and a sense of companionship are usually more important than the topic of conversation.

A generous way of viewing small talk as a phenomenon is that it's the neurotypical's attempt at infodumping — which starts but then stops. Your NT conversation partner may, for instance, want to talk about the weather, but stops before getting to anything truly interesting. One strategy could be to take them at their word and initiate a deep conversation about meteorological phenomena. This is likely not going to be appreciated, however, as the most important rule for small talk is that it shouldn't mean anything.

As an autist, it's a good idea to learn a few phrases; these will come in handy. See the glossary for some suggestions. It's harder to establish a good connection with neurotypicals if you haven't engaged in chitchat first.

For an autistic person, small talk is challenging. We want to participate, but we can't. This inability has nothing to do with arrogance, but since neurotypicals may assume so, you might as well memorise a few lines that you can use.

Small talk rarely contains anything of interest. Autists would rather get straight to the point and talk about things that matter or get to know the other person more deeply.

To understand small talk, you need to remember that neurotypicals communicate for other purposes than simply to exchange information. For them, seemingly empty chitchat actually serves a purpose. It's a way of probing, of testing the waters. They use small talk to form a sense of the person they are talking to. The topic of discussion is unimportant; it usually ends up being whatever is closest at hand, like the weather, or the coffee maker at work. The purpose of small talk is to pinpoint who the other person is. It is, in fact, a rather intricate game.

The difficulty for the autist is that this game contains too many layers of pretence. You need to talk and keep the conversation flowing, without uttering anything that could be perceived as the least bit controversial or as a promise. It should be pleasant and insincere, all while you are also being scrutinised and judged. You have to keep track of facial expressions and body language, and manage to talk without saying anything. In other words, it's utterly draining. The autist bends over backwards and eventually gets tongue-tied.

The peculiar thing about neurotypicals is that they are simultaneously preoccupied with other people and with distancing themselves. They maintain a facade and avoid getting too close. At the same time, they care a

great deal what others think. Many of them don't seem
to see this as a contradiction but entirely normal.

GLOSSARY

'**All right, then**' or '**It was nice seeing you**' can mean 'I want to end our conversation.'

'**We should get together soon for coffee/lunch**' might also mean they won't be in touch.

'**Everything is going to be fine.**' Neurotypicals say this to comfort others, even though they can't possibly know what the future holds.

'**Tell me EVERYTHING!**' They don't mean everything. They mean, 'Give me a summary of what happened, focusing on the most important, funniest, and surprising parts.'

'**How are you?**' 'In what sense, and compared to when?' the autist wonders, wanting to give an honest, exhaustive answer. There is no need. Just reply, 'Good, and you?' This phrase is just noise, not a genuine question.

Autistic voices

Casimir: 'I'm not very good at small talk or conversations with other people that aren't strictly necessary in the moment. Yet my neurotypical brother voluntarily goes to summer camp.'

Henrik: 'Everyone wants a personal, emotional connection to someone. A relationship. The perplexing thing about neurotypicals is that they then work so hard to distance themselves from their relationships. They don't want to talk about deep things. They want to connect with someone but they simultaneously make a real effort *not* to. I want to engage in an interesting conversation about something personal and deep, something rewarding and enriching.'

Elli: 'I don't understand people who talk without having anything to say. Do they think without having any thoughts, too?'

Anna: 'When it's time for small talk or gossip among people who don't know me well, I pretend. Somehow, I seem to bring something out in most people, a kind of trust. Don't ask me how; I don't know. They usually start discussing deeper thoughts, feelings, and opinions with me pretty quickly. And then I can stop pretending.'

Elli: 'It's incomprehensible how it can be interesting to sit and talk about what you did during the day, what others said, what you had for lunch today or yesterday, empty prattle about what you'll be up to this weekend and what you did last weekend. How this can serve as "social glue" is beyond me.'

Emma: 'I hear so many people complain about everyday photos, food pics, and boring posts on social media. Then you step out into the real world — and what are people talking about? That's it, the exact same things.'

Tobias: 'I'm perfectly capable of seeing for myself what the weather is like.'

Lying

Now we come to one of the most challenging things about neurotypicals. They think it's normal to lie. Not only do they tell lies themselves, but they also expect others to lie to them.

They often say that lying is wrong, but they don't mean it. Certain lies are accepted because they are deemed necessary. These are called 'white lies'.

NTs use white lies to avoid hurting someone or to refrain from sharing something they think might be too much for the other person to bear.

They may tell themselves that lying is kind and considerate. They imagine that untruths used for positive effect don't count as lies.

If, for instance, an NT wants to encourage a nervous and anxious person, they might say: 'You'll do great!' Of course, they can't know that for sure. They don't consider that the recipient might take them at their word and interpret it as a promise, only to be disappointed if the statement doesn't come true.

The less well you know the person you are interacting with, the more acceptable it is to lie. For instance, many find it perfectly fine to lie to someone you meet on a dating app but aren't interested in. If so, you can in good conscience come up with an excuse to cut the date short. Your pet is sick, you have to get up early to travel the next day, you need to meet a friend to hand over their keys — anything goes. Most people wouldn't think you are in the wrong.

Being impolite or clumsy is considered worse than lying. For this reason, neurotypicals would rather lie than risk hurting someone.

They often assume the truth hurts. If they are annoyed with an autist, they might refrain from saying so because they think the other person will get upset. They don't realise that the autist would prefer to hear the truth and often has no problem handling it.

The mistake we autists make is assuming that everyone communicates sincerely. For us, truth, authenticity, and thoroughness are important, and we assume everyone else functions that way too. We share information the same way we would like to receive it — honestly and comprehensively.

This rarely goes down well with neurotypicals.

If you want to make a neurotypical happy, you are better off not answering honestly to questions about their private life, clothes, weight, or family. These questions generally aren't meant as honest inquiries, but rather as requests for praise.

Being tactful is slightly different from lying. Tact means knowing when it's okay to speak your mind and in which situations it's better to stay silent. It can also mean trying to sugarcoat your answer. For example, take the question, **'Did you like the food I made?'** There are several possible answers:

'**No, I did not.**' The truth.

'**Brussels sprouts aren't usually my favourite, but the combination with the omelette was interesting.**' A tactful way of shifting focus.

'**Yes, it was yummy.**' A white lie.

However, neurotypicals may mistake dishonesty for showing tact. They can be so afraid of the truth that they think lying is more tactful than telling it like it is. Here, they assume a right they don't really have: deciding what's best for the person being lied to.

Lying through flattery is also an accepted way to

navigate the social landscape. Neurotypicals may give compliments in order to climb the social hierarchy in the group they want to be part of. Similarly, they may speak ill of others and spread false rumours to lower someone else's status.

Falling victim to gossip can be devastating since many neurotypicals judge people they don't know based on what others say about them, instead of what they know from personal experience.

In a TED talk, the developmental researcher Kang Lee says that children are instinctive liars and lying is a normal part of their development. This is not true. Some children lie more than others, and autistic children lie less frequently than their neurotypical peers. It's just as 'normal' not to lie; the difference is that the truth-tellers are fewer than the liars.

Lee has studied children all over the world. So why do a majority of children lie but not all? he asks. Good lying requires good ingredients, just like cooking, he says. One such ingredient is theory of mind, Lee explains, which is the 'ability to know that different people have different knowledge about a situation'.

The children who lie the earliest and with the highest degree of sophistication are those with the most advanced ability to read others' minds. These are skills we need to function well in society, Lee says. 'So, if you discover your two-year-old telling his or her first lie, instead of being alarmed, you should celebrate!' he urges his audience. 'It signals that your child has arrived at a new milestone of typical development.'

His conclusion is that children who lie the most have progressed furthest in their development. The 10 to 20 per cent of children who rarely or never lie aren't mentioned in his talk.

Not uttering a word about the immorality of lying and deception is, of course, preposterous. Lee's TED talk is like a satire of our era's survival-of-the-fittest culture, where everything is a matter of self-interest and facade.

Most of the time, neurotypicals don't mean any harm when they mislead you or tell white lies. They may want to protect you from the truth, and they do this out of goodwill. To them, the truth can hurt if it threatens their belief system, so they would prefer to avoid it. But autists often prefer the truth.

This doesn't mean that autists can't lie. We can. We just aren't very good at it.

Neurotypicals lie in order to:

- avoid conflict or hurting someone
- gain power
- downplay problems and mistakes
- exaggerate their own importance.

For neurotypicals, the hierarchy of a group is important. Who is the leader, and who is at the bottom? They like to establish these things quickly. Some people are elevated and popular in certain settings, such as the family, classroom, friendship group, workplace, or even the world.

Neurotypicals struggle to decide for themselves who should be the leader. Instead, they echo what they perceive to be others' opinions and pay attention to those they feel are ranked more highly than themselves. Money, looks, and physical strength can all affect a person's status within a group.

Have you ever noticed that sometimes neurotypicals praise or criticise an idea depending on who suggests it? The very same idea elicits different reactions based on who's talking. This is because NTs don't just assess the idea itself; they also consider the status of the person who came up with it. For them, this is as important as

all — I could share my flaws without caring if people judged me. I have a core deep inside me that no one can reach and where no one can touch me. And so it doesn't matter what others think or say. That's how I have felt and thought. But over time, I have become a bit more cautious. I have noticed that my sincerity can affect me negatively.

Humour is a common survival strategy for autists. Making fun of your own shortcomings can turn into a kind of defence mechanism. To take the sting out of things you are afraid will seem odd, you joke about them. The key is to be first — to make fun of yourself before someone else does. It's not hard, and there is plenty of material. Misunderstandings that arise in communication with neurotypicals are often funny. As are literal interpretations and peculiar associations.

Many autists are good at making others laugh; humour often lives in the details, and that's our area of expertise. We are also used to spotting patterns in human behaviour, and there is a lot of good material there, too.

Often, we don't even have to try to be funny; all we need to do is be ourselves.

But being the class clown can also be dangerous. The weaknesses you share in jest can be used against you.

They can become valuable ammunition for those who want to speak ill of you. And being indifferent about your reputation may seem suspicious to neurotypicals who are very concerned about their own.

GLOSSARY

Food or drink tasting 'different' not only means that the taste is unexpected; the neurotypical doesn't like it.

Someone being 'special' or 'different' isn't just a description of a person but can also mean that the neurotypical in question is suspicious of them.

When you give an NT a present and they say, 'You didn't have to do that', it doesn't mean they don't want the gift. On the contrary, they are grateful to be remembered and a bit embarrassed by the attention.

'Would you be so kind as to close the window?' The sentence means you are being asked to close the window. The question isn't about whether you, as a person, are kind.

Autistic voices

Fabian: 'After you've lied, you feel awful.'

Teodor: 'They're so two-faced in how they talk. They'll say one thing but do the opposite. They'll go on about liking or disliking someone, but then their actions paint a completely different picture. And they'll give out advice, declaring how things should be, without practising what they preach.'

Naomi: 'They ask questions they don't really want an answer to — they only want a specific answer.'

Michaela: 'In school last Monday, my teacher asked if I'd had a good weekend. When I replied, "No, I accidentally deleted a character in a game I'd spent 30 hours building and got really angry," she seemed very uncomfortable. We didn't speak again that day.'

Fabian: 'Neurotypicals seem better at being anyone or anything.'

Charlotte: 'My mother is an autist's worst nightmare. Forget about clear communication — it's prohibited because it's "impolite". Everything always has to be sugarcoated. When I lived with her, I wanted to do my own laundry. But every time I asked her to show me how the washing machine works, she'd say, "I'll do your laundry." So, I never got to do it. If I asked her when the laundry would be done, she'd let out this big sigh, as if I was "pressuring her". I really just wanted to know when the laundry would be done so I could plan my outfits. Ideally, I would have preferred to do the laundry myself, but I didn't know what to say or do that would result in her showing me how the machine worked.'

Michaela: 'We were hanging a sign over the door. The person doing the hanging turned to me and asked, "Is it straight?" I looked at it and said "No" before walking away. I heard them laughing down the corridor, and later I found out she had wanted me to straighten the sign. If she had said so, I would have done it, of course.'

Linnéa: 'If someone close to me asks a question, and I get the feeling they're not really interested in hearing the truth, I will say: "Do you want an honest answer? If not, don't ask me. I'll answer honestly or not at all." With acquaintances or people I barely know, I try to guess what they want to hear, to avoid hurting them. I don't like lying, though, not even out of politeness.

'It's tricky when I'm the one asking. I expect honesty but often I'm met with these polite responses. So I always clarify: "Please, tell me the truth; I'm asking because I want an honest answer."'

Holly: 'My friend and I, we loved the same band and used to go to their concerts together every time they played. It was our thing. We hadn't seen each other in a long time; she had moved in with her partner, relocated to a new city, and picked up new hobbies — replacing her old life with a new one. So, I was thrilled when I heard that our band was coming to Sweden again. It was a perfect chance for us to catch up! I shot her a message and asked if she wanted to go with me.

'"Oh, fun!" she replied, but thought she might be busy — what a bummer.

'"I see," I said, "but the concert is more than six months away. Can't you rearrange your plans?"

'"Yeah, but work might be an issue, I'm not sure I'll be able to take time off," she replied.

'And I wrote that, surely, she must be allowed *one* day off? I got quite worked up on her behalf. What boss would deny you a single day off more than six months in advance when you have a desk job? I worried about her work environment — it didn't sound good at all — but she didn't elaborate on that.

'Then there was the money, she said; she couldn't afford to buy a ticket. I know they own a house, have well-paid jobs and a nice car, and the tickets weren't that expensive — but since I'm not privy to their personal finances, I didn't want to assume. I also didn't want to ask, since it can be a touchy subject.

'Instead, I wrote and offered to cover her ticket, so she wouldn't have to worry about that. It was a lot of money for me, because I was on sick leave at the time. But I didn't tell her that, of course — it was worth every penny to see her again.

'That's when she lost it. "WHY CAN'T YOU UNDERSTAND THAT I DON'T WANT TO

GO TO THAT BLOODY CONCERT," she wrote in all caps. And that it was mean of me to continue to pressure her.

'I was flabbergasted, and asked why she didn't say so from the start. She replied that she didn't want to hurt my feelings. She said that's what people do, and I should stop playing dumb. People lie so as not to make others sad. She was very angry with me — she said she didn't like lying, but I had forced her to do so by being so clueless. Somehow, it ended up being my fault that she'd lied.'

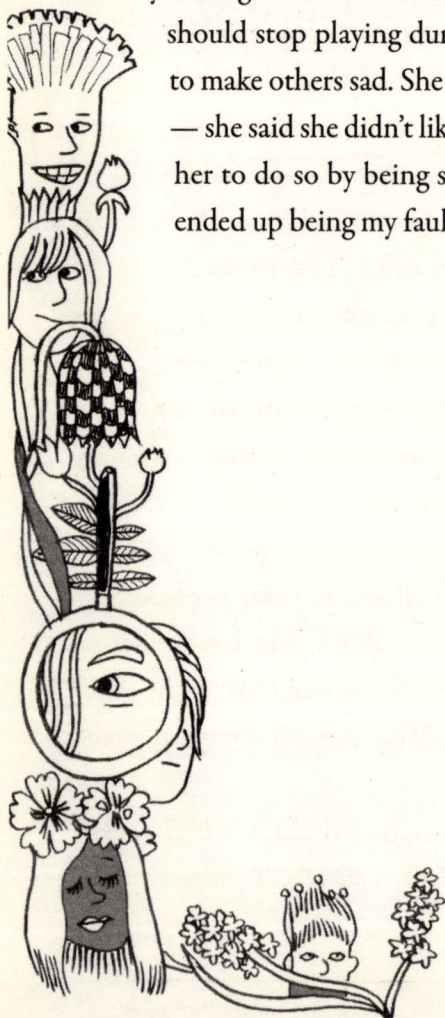

Insensitive to sensory stimuli

'You're so sensitive!' As an autist, you have probably heard this comment from a neurotypical at some point or other. Neurotypicals can be very sensitive too, but in their own way.

They are not hypersensitive to sensory stimuli. This allows them to wear uncomfortable clothes that chafe their skin. They aren't bothered by the refrigerator's humming, noisy cars, or a fellow passenger on the train speaking loudly on their phone. If they even notice the noise, they can tune it out. They can endure bright light without sunglasses, aren't troubled by strong smells, and appear indifferent to temperature changes.

They don't get up in the middle of the night to change sheets because the ones they have made the bed with are pilling and feel uncomfortable against their skin. They aren't aware of every single movement they make and the feelings in them. When they punch in a code, grasp a doorhandle, press it down, pull to open the door, feel the draft as it swings open, and hold it so it doesn't slam shut too hard behind them, they don't register the sensation of the surfaces against their palm and the muscles in their hand and arms. They simply open and let go of the door, automatically, without thinking about what they are doing.

They can walk past a fragrant flower without stopping to bury their nose in it. If they receive an unwanted hug, pat on the shoulder, or slap on the back, it doesn't linger in their body for hours; they can shrug it off and forget all about it a moment later.

This may seem sad. Neurotypicals miss out on the child's view of the world and strong, immediate experiences. They read books about mindfulness and practise being in the here and now. Being present in the moment is a state they often claim to long for.

Still, there are also advantages to their lack of sensitivity, and to their use of signs and symbols. It allows them to function well in groups, which helps them form strong cultures. During a conversation, neurotypicals can both hear what's being said and process the meaning of the words. At the same time as they are sensing the speaker's intention and other nuances, they can read facial expressions and notice other things happening in the room.

How can they do so much at once? It's quite astonishing — and all because they filter their stimuli. They aren't struck by the full force of sensory impressions but only register a minimum of symbols. They can balance their attention. For this reason, they aren't as easily distracted by things such as loud background noise or multiple parallel conversations in the same room.

Many neurotypicals associate light and darkness with emotional states. Light is linked to happiness, and darkness to sadness. This is why neurotypicals like to turn on the light if they find you in a dark room. They do this out of care, as they are worried that the darkness might be bringing you down.

They may also struggle with poor night vision and cannot imagine that you might be enjoying the gloom. They don't need to recover from overwhelming sensory stimuli like we do. Consequently, they only sit in dark rooms when they are sick or going to sleep. A sudden strong light doesn't cause them pain as they aren't hypersensitive to sensory stimuli, so they will likely think your reaction is exaggerated.

If you can't get a neurotypical in your life to stop

turning on the light, a tip might be to simply unscrew or unplug it.

Things neurotypicals *are* hypersensitive to:

- If you aren't making eye contact.
- If you want to be left alone.
- If you don't participate in a conversation.
- If you use the wrong tone when you speak.
- If you don't want them to touch you.
- If you don't want to eat certain foods.
- If you wear earplugs or ear defenders among people.
- If you are stimming in public.
- If you don't adhere to the same traditions as they do.
- If you question their authority.
- If you correct them when they say or spell something wrong.
- If you speak the truth when you shouldn't.
- If you share too many facts they didn't ask for.
- If you ask them to be quiet, as their talk is distracting and overwhelming.

Many neurotypicals can be sensitive to hearing too much about your special interest. Of course, it can be considered rude not to ask your conversation partner *anything* about their life, but NTs can also feel threatened when you know more than they do about a particular topic.

Some neurotypicals have zero tolerance for social clumsiness, as they believe that others act with ulterior motives or hidden malicious intent. Some of them are extremely easily offended. When I once told my NT boyfriend that his quirks (in my opinion, hypochondria) made him a difficult person, he sulked for days. It made no difference that I tried to present it as a judgement-free statement that didn't mean I loved him any less. Nor did it help when I explained that I, too, am very difficult. You weren't allowed to say that, he thought.

In the eyes of some NTs, it's rude to share any facts at all unless your conversation partner explicitly asks. Good advice can be perceived as 'shaming'. Being clumsy is no excuse, as neurotypicals assume that all people are manipulative.

Because a convivial atmosphere in the group is more important to them than the actual content of a conversation, they will get bored if they don't get to participate. It doesn't matter to them if they don't know anything about the topic; they still aren't satisfied just listening — they also need to speak.

If you are too quiet in a conversation, neurotypicals may think you 'aren't contributing'. All the while you probably think that you are listening and will speak when you feel that you have something to say.

Autistic voices

Carolina: 'For my sister's birthday, I thought I'd draw a portrait of her — I'm an artist and she's always going on about how much she loves my art. The portrait turned out very lifelike, and I was quite pleased with it. But the next day, my mum called and asked how I could be so cruel to my sister, humiliating her in front of everyone. Now she was devastated and thought I didn't like her.

'I didn't understand at all.

'I told a painter friend what had happened and asked if it was really such a bad portrait. He said the problem was that it was *too* lifelike. I had drawn her the way she looks, with all her lines and wrinkles. I thought it was natural, since she's over 50 and that's her face. But apparently, people don't want to be portrayed the way they look. My friend said I should have made her look

20 years younger, and a bit slimmer, but I thought that sounded ridiculous.'

Sara: 'When my neurotypical partner sprains his foot and can't walk, for example, he doesn't want advice on how to heal quicker or how to stop it from happening again. All he really wants is for me to sympathise and say I feel bad for him. I've learned this makes him feel better.'

Casimir: 'I realise I'm different, but it's never been a problem for me.'

Rules are rules

It's crucial to understand that some neurotypicals pretend there are strict rules to follow when it comes to social interaction. They talk about 'unspoken rules' that everyone is expected to know.

But in reality, the rules constantly change according to a complicated and inconsistent system. An autistic person could labour their whole life to learn the rules, but since these rules are ever-changing, they will always lag behind.

One of the most challenging aspects of adulthood is first learning what rules apply, and then understanding when it's okay to break them. Here, neurotypicals are often inconsistent and unreliable. If they consider certain rules and agreements to be inconsequential, they break them all the time. This can be arbitrary and difficult to predict. It happens so often, you can scarcely say there are any rules at all.

For example, grown-ups may teach children to say thank you, not to lie, and that they don't have to hug strangers. Later in life, children are taught to make exceptions to these rules depending on the context. For instance, saying thank you too many times may be perceived as unnerving, their friends may get upset if they speak the truth too freely, and they are expected to hug relatives whom they barely know.

If you ask neurotypicals to explain a social rule, you might get answers such as:

'Conversations don't always have a purpose.'

'It's just a matter of being polite and friendly.'

'It depends on the situation.'

'You have to learn to pick up on the signals.'

In other words, there aren't really any hard and fast rules.

But back in the day, there used to be more. In some ways it was a simpler time, as people were largely in agreement on common ways of expressing themselves. You were supposed to show respect when addressing your elders, superiors, or people you didn't know; and you could learn good manners and etiquette as well as polite phrases that everyone used. Today these phrases have all but disappeared, as we have decided that they are old-fashioned and a sign of inequality. What's perceived as friendly manners today is much more vague and diffuse, and thus harder to memorise.

Since neurotypicals don't find rules to be important, they can get angry if you point out that they have broken one. If you report them for breaking a rule when it didn't harm anyone, they can get very upset and think that you are disloyal and a tattletale.

Autistic voices

Simon: 'They insist on all these behavioural rules but don't follow them. Like being on time — but then most people don't bother with it.'

Hanna: 'They're always so unclear about what's been decided, it drives me nuts.'

Erika: 'I don't get it. If you're talking about doing something at a later date, why is it so hard for people to just say, "Let's do activity X at time Y in place Z"? Instead, there's all this enthusiasm but no plans. Then I have to be the awkward control freak insisting on finalising the details.'

Karin: 'They struggle with clear instructions. If I ask them to clarify or be more specific, they don't understand how and just end up repeating what they've already said. If I give them clear instructions, they don't follow them to the letter but only kind of — even if they know it's important to me that they do it exactly right.'

Starting and stopping

Have you ever been called spoiled or ungrateful for not coming to the dinner table when others were waiting? Maybe your parent has cooked your favourite meal, but you can't tear yourself away from the game or book you are engrossed in.

As autists, we tend to 'lock in' on what we are doing and be a bit more set in our thoughts and interests than others. This is because we can hyperfocus and enter such deep concentration that it takes a while to break.

To other people, it may seem like we are self-centred. We are not. Being self-centred means believing you are more important than others. We don't think that. But it takes us longer to shift focus.

While an autistic person needs to think their way through life, neurotypicals can do lots of things on

autopilot, without needing to think. This makes them flexible and open to change. They can quickly switch between different tasks. They change plans without being negatively affected. Many can live their lives under a great deal of stress without seeming to suffer from it.

Yet there is an exception, and that's in times of crisis. If something completely upends the neurotypical's existence — such as an unexpected death or illness, or losing a job — then problems pile up.

In such situations, neurotypicals may break down or become paralysed, as they didn't expect what's happening. Suddenly, they are without a ready-made category to place the event in.

To an autist, then, neurotypicals seem highly sensitive to setbacks. Autists are used to not having ready-made categories and to living with the understanding that each situation is unique.

Those who always struggle with what's easy for others get used to being in a sort of permanent crisis. For this reason, many autists are good at keeping calm and thinking clearly in bigger crises. They can often act quickly and rationally and be of support to neurotypicals.

Demands for change

Neurotypicals like change, as long as it doesn't threaten their status in the group. They see things changing as a sign of success and improvement. It's as though variety were an end in itself. Even if they have found their favourite dish, for instance, they may want to cook or order another, different dish just to 'try something new'. To them, the novelty is more important than what they actually enjoy the most.

They also like being close to others. Since they aren't hypersensitive to sensory stimuli, they enjoy noise and crowds. If you are recommending a restaurant to a neurotypical, you would do well to choose a lively place with lots of people. They aren't necessarily bothered by the din; on the contrary, they feel safe, as a bustling environment indicates that the restaurant is popular with others. They are also less likely to be faced with silence, which they tend to find uncomfortable.

Neurotypicals are often afraid of being perceived as socially deviant and may refrain from doing things they actually want to do for fear of what others might think. In today's society, the ideal is to put yourself first and prioritise your own independent choices, but neurotypicals don't tend to practise what they preach in this department. They claim to strive for good habits, but in reality they often get bored with their own fixed routines.

NTs like surprises. They find it exciting not to know what's going to happen; they get a kick out of uncertainty. If you want to make a neurotypical happy, you could take them somewhere they haven't been before. A person who wants to prepare before going to a new place could seem dull to an NT. Many of them prefer unpredictability.

Some even get so bored with the lack of excitement in everyday life that they seek to 'challenge themselves' through various physical feats such as climbing mountains or cycling long distances. To someone for whom it's a daily challenge to simply put one foot in front of the other, it might seem absurd that others want to create difficulties for themselves.

Autists often have a rich inner world and an ability to entertain ourselves. We easily find things to contemplate and don't need as much external stimulation. It may look as though we are just staring into space, but on the inside we are full of activity. We rarely get bored of our own company.

Neurotypicals don't train as hard as we do simply to exist in the world. They don't need to mask their difficulties because society is built for them. Things happen automatically for them; they don't need to consciously learn things like social interaction.

They can, of course, feel terrible and have lots of problems and conditions that complicate their life, but their neurotypicality always brings certain advantages (which they are rarely aware of) compared to autists.

They don't try as hard to understand us as we do to understand them. They don't adapt to us. They don't have to, as they are in the majority.

Young autistic people often get drilled in good manners. There are some who, with good intentions, want to teach autists 'how to behave'. The problem with that, though, is that in their effort to demonstrate how to be a perfect person, these people set unreasonable demands. The autist is to be trained to a level of social agility and fine-tuned sensitivity that is rarely required of those who aren't deemed to need to learn it. Requirements may be added that few others live up to.

For example, I once listened to a radio interview with an autistic woman who was a lecturer. She sought help from a well-meaning neurotypical who was going to teach her to consider how best to present. There were all these dress codes the autist was expected to follow. Open-toed shoes weren't appropriate for lecturing, nor tank tops. Suddenly, the demands on the autist were very high, yet she accepted everything she was told about how she should look.

But many neurotypicals don't live according to such 'musts' at all; they may very well lecture in a tank top. They don't rigorously follow dress codes. (Even when they probably should.)

My point is: You don't have to be perfect. You try hard every day, and that's enough. The NT ideal of a completely faultless friend, colleague, or partner isn't something they embody themselves. It's precisely that — an *ideal*, not anchored in reality. The following is enough: say thank you, apologise if you have wronged someone, treat others as you would want to be treated, and don't use your way of functioning as an excuse to behave badly. However, your way of functioning *can* serve as an explanation for why you do things differently.

If you pay too much attention to neurotypicals who want to change you, it can damage your self-esteem, and you may become so amenable to others' will that you erase yourself. NTs often mean well but are a little arrogant in their belief that everyone is like them and that their way of doing things is always best.

But there is also an important advantage to all the time you, as an autist, spend learning about social interaction. All that practice allows you to get to know yourself. You know how you function, what you need, what triggers and soothes you, what you like, and what you don't like. This may sound obvious, but far from every neurotypical knows themselves all that well. They don't understand their own reactions, impulses, weaknesses, strengths, and feelings. If you don't know where such things come from, you can neither communicate your needs to others nor make changes to feel better.

They haven't had to put in the same hard work. But you have. So you know a lot about yourself.

Knowing yourself is a great asset when forming relationships. It allows you to tell the other person how you function and what you need. Just by doing that, you have laid the foundation for a mutual understanding. Of course, the opposite is also true: you need to listen to what the other person tells you about themselves and be able to compromise.

Sometimes people say that being autistic is a superpower. It may not often feel that way when you live with autism every day. But do you know what *is* a superpower? *Knowing* you are autistic.

You can't change something you aren't aware of or don't want to admit. But things you know, you can use to parry and avoid difficult situations. Above all, you can manage and conserve your energy.

Stop, breathe, and feel. Squeeze your fidget toy, put on your favourite song in your headphones and play it over and over again, find a quiet place, don't talk, think. Wait and breathe. Then, act.

Must we understand them?

'In a perfect world, [...] I wouldn't have to learn how to word things so a neurotypical person doesn't find offence where there is none to be taken. But we don't live in a perfect world,' says Kassandra, an autistic participant on the Netflix reality series *Love on the Spectrum*.

She is right. The world isn't perfect. We autists aren't judged fairly and understood, even though we should be. To live in this world, we must adapt. This is because neurotypicals outnumber us by so many. Life is easier if you are neurotypical. Anything else would be a lie.

But must we really put so much energy into understanding the way neurotypicals think? Yes and no. If you want to, you can view NTs negatively, of course, as needy clones full of prejudice and preconceived notions. But we'll encounter them in all aspects of life and have much to gain from understanding them.

This doesn't mean you should deny your true self and live your life behind a mask. Trying to suppress your autism is a terrible way to live, sapping your strength and leading to anxiety and depression. It never works in the long run. Autism always catches up with you.

The point isn't for you to adapt to them. But to get the most out of life, you'll need to relate to their way of functioning because most teachers, friends, colleagues, employers, neighbours, and other acquaintances you encounter will be neurotypical. Smoother interactions with them can help you get the life you want.

It doesn't mean you should change or try to be someone you are not, only that you need to be prepared for what lies ahead.

TIPS: EVERYDAY LIFE

When you move out, get a simple home. Don't buy too many things and pets; go easy on the interior design projects. Don't renovate. However, a few things that matter: If you have difficulty showering because the stream hurts your skin and the transition between hot and cold is painful, make sure there is a bathtub. If brushing your teeth is a challenge and your electric toothbrush is too loud, buy one that's battery powered — they are less noisy. Stim toys and your own quiet corner are good investments. Weighted blankets and shoes without laces are great, too. You can also try using a clothes rack where, once a week, you select and hang up clothes for the next seven days.

If you live in a city and can afford it, pay for cleaning services and subscribe to a meal delivery plan. If you can't, create a cleaning schedule where you don't do everything at once but divide up the tasks on different days. Monday, bathroom; Tuesday, vacuuming; etc.

Also, make a meal schedule for every day of the week, including a list of ingredients to buy. Follow the schedule religiously; it relieves the brain. You can also do meal prep in lunch boxes; that way you only need to cook once a week.

Free AI services such as Goblin Tools can help you break down big projects that feel overwhelming into smaller parts. This tool also creates a to-do list for each task.

Lean into JOMO — the joy of missing out. Stay home. Don't buy into the myth that you have to rush around from one activity to the next to be a modern person. Shrink your life to fit you, get rid of stuff and obligations, and protect everything that makes you feel good. Dare to opt out of bigger settings. You don't have to endure everything. Just do what you like and at your own pace.

Sure, nutrients are important, but eating the same thing often won't kill you. Don't feel ashamed if you dine from a limited repertoire. In this era, people are obsessively fixated on health, food, and dietary advice. It's perfectly fine to survive on sandwiches. 'Samefoods' are cosy and comforting. Not everything has to be varied endlessly. The advantage of products like crackers, potato chips, and crispbread is their predictability; they taste the same every time. Fruit and vegetables, on the other hand, can taste completely different depending on the season, ripeness, temperature, etc. It's not so strange if you would rather avoid them.

Be a little suspicious of services that claim to teach everyday structure and how to manage a home. Remember that order and structure are special interests for people running such businesses and services. This makes them masters of creating new obligations that you didn't even know existed. It can add to your burden rather than simplify life. I have rarely felt so overwhelmed as when I tried to view a so-called 'model apartment' that was used as a showcase for people with neurodevelopmental conditions. The kitchen alone was full of signs with instructions and admonitions I had never even thought of. I stumbled out of there feeling like even more of a failure than before — I, who don't clean the kitchen fan and have no sorting system for dry goods.

Autistic voices

Lenka: 'They keep their schedules jam-packed with activities, trips, and social gatherings. Not a day goes by without something in the calendar. At work, they like to talk about all their adventures and holidays. But me? My calendar is usually empty, no planned trips. No daily activities. Do I want to come to the party? No thanks, I'll be recuperating. I need some peace and quiet, some time to unwind — maybe catch up on some reading. I need to recharge my batteries to be ready for work again.'

Henrik: 'I've noticed they can't stand being away from work. Even when they're sick, they say it's so hard because they're itching to get back. But, what? Like, are you crazy? It's fine, I can stay home. No problem. I'd gladly stay home for the rest of my life.'

Ira: 'I want to talk about what it's like being an autist in Sweden who's from another country. I'm always wrestling with it. Like, if I want to voice my frustration and try to do it the "Swedish way" — you know, gently and soft-spoken — nobody takes me seriously. But if I'm more direct about my needs without being rude, I still come off that way. And then they ask why I didn't say anything earlier. It drives me crazy; it's impossible to get it right.'

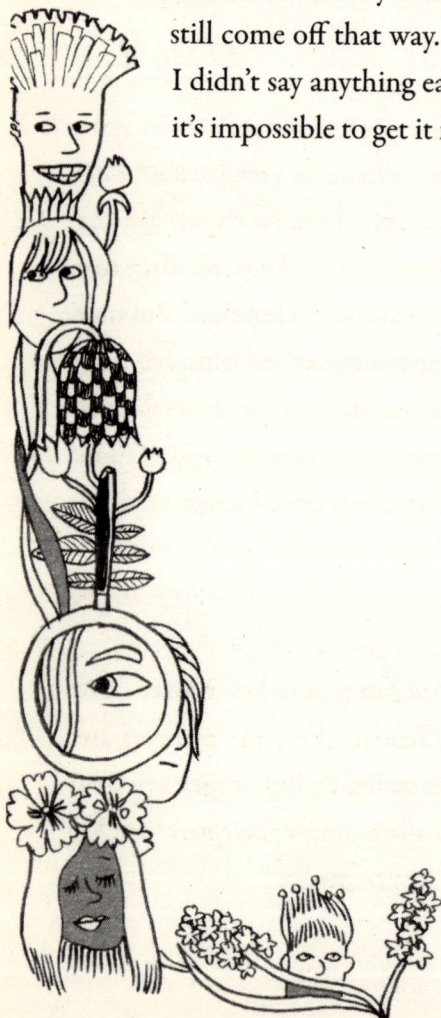

General interests

Neurotypicals rarely develop true special interests. Sure, they too can be interested in things like Greek mythology, octopuses, the Tudors, Morse code, or anime — but their interests are often of a more temporary, general kind. This is because they get bored quickly. They can have interests but are seldom wholly absorbed by them. Often, they aren't willing to invest the time required to become truly knowledgeable about a subject. After a while, they tire and start longing for company and variety.

Some neurotypicals may even pretend to be interested in something just to be part of the group — especially if it involves a group activity. What's most important to them is to be in the same place as and engaging with others, not what they do together. Their interest may just as well spring from their membership in a group as from within themselves.

Watching a TV series or a film together with an NT can be difficult. They may struggle to immerse themselves in the story and fully concentrate on the images, music, and dialogue. They don't let themselves be enveloped and absorbed. Many want to talk while they watch or pause the film to get snacks. They may also have difficulty remembering lines from the film or series afterwards. It's as if they don't really care about it.

One reason for their lack of special interests is that they are rarely as detail oriented as autists. They fail to notice the little things because their focus is on the bigger picture. They forget names, can't recall what's been said in a conversation, and miss important details that — for them — are lost in the totality. This can make it difficult for them to be precise. Everything bleeds into everything else, turning into a kind of soup when they communicate. Since the demand for detailed knowledge in school and at work is low, they don't see this as a problem.

They may think the autistic preoccupation with details is odd, perceiving them as unnecessary. A secondary or trivial matter. What they rarely understand is that what begins as a detail tends to end in the bigger picture when an autist hyperfocuses on their special interest.

Think about it. Suppose that your special interest,

as an autist, is the Mexican axolotl. You learn the Latin names of all the species of the mole salamander genus.

Here, neurotypicals in your surroundings may think this is unnecessary knowledge that you have no 'use' for. But you have only scratched the surface. Keep going! Go into even more detail. Learn how the water temperature and oxygen levels affect the interplay between lungs, gills, and skin when the axolotl breathes; study the ancient system of channels and lakes near Mexico City that makes up the axolotl's habitat; and learn about the Aztec language Nahuatl, from which the name 'axolotl' originates. Now you have touched on more general knowledge of biology, ecology, and history. Keep going! Delve into the International Union for Conservation of Nature's work on red-listing endangered plant and animal species.

And what's happened now? Well, you have broken through from the level of extreme detail to the general. Your knowledge has expanded. Step by step, by gathering and piecing together details, you have completed the puzzle. The big picture — the whole — has emerged.

It's a time-consuming way to acquire knowledge, but it's comprehensive. Most neurotypicals don't have the patience. They read some general information and form a rough idea.

Those who, like the autist, gather a lot of information also discover patterns. Autists are often referred to as 'pattern seekers' or 'pattern finders'. And what is a pattern, if not a kind of whole?

Even if we don't automatically or intuitively understand certain aspects of human behaviour, we can learn by gathering information about what others feel, think, and do. Then we can weigh, measure, and construct probabilities and scenarios around it. Suddenly, a larger pattern emerges. And perhaps we have noticed something that has eluded others.

Because neurotypicals don't think details are crucial, they can be sensitive to being corrected about things they perceive as 'trivial'. It's not as important to them to get it right. In their eyes, the most important thing is not to lose face. If you say, 'A banana is not a fruit but a berry', they feel criticised and attacked, as if you have told them they are stupid.

TIPS: FRIENDSHIP

Find other autists. Seek out other autistic individuals and find support. Listen to others' experiences and advice. Don't compare yourself to neurotypicals. They operate on another frequency. Most likely, you won't find the same things as they do difficult, boring, or tiring.

Surround yourself with open-minded people — both in friendship and in love. If neurotypicals interpret you as speaking with a subtext when you aren't, or get inexplicably annoyed with you, ask them what just happened. Explain how you function. It may be difficult for them to grasp, but if, after several attempts, you aren't being heard, it may be time to question the relationship.

The number of friends you have truly doesn't matter. Choose them with care.

Don't listen to claims that autism is being exaggerated. This assertion stems from ignorance and comes from people who can't tolerate that not everyone is like them. The reason autism is talked about more today is partly that our knowledge has increased, and partly that society has become more streamlined and demanding, making autists more visible, as we stand out more.

Neither should you heed those who, in the belief that they are being tolerant and broad-minded, want to deny your difference. In reality, they are engaging in a form of erasure.

How do you distinguish between banter among friends and bullying? The following are not okay:

- teasing, belittling, or calling someone names 'as a joke'
- hitting or groping
- threatening
- lying about someone, spreading gossip, or revealing secrets
- stealing something that belongs to someone else
- excluding another person.

Social conditioning for neurotypicals

(or, how to get an autist to like you)

- Reduce eye contact during conversations.

- Only ask questions if you want a detailed and honest answer.

- Say exactly what you mean. Don't drop hints. Don't hide things, and don't assume something is 'implied' or 'obvious'.

- Do talk about a specific subject rather than engaging in small talk.

- Allow for associations. Don't be afraid of background details and digressions.

- Remember that a conversation can never contain too many exciting facts.

- Show empathy by sharing your own experiences and personal anecdotes related to what you are discussing. Doing so is not self-centred.

- Be reliable and don't break agreements, no matter how small and trivial they may seem to you. If you have promised to show up at 10 am with two bananas, don't get there at 10.15 with three apples.

- Dare to go deep and give generously of yourself. Don't hide behind a facade.

- Assist with practical tasks that come automatically to you.

- If you are with an autistic person who is shutting down or experiencing a meltdown, let them be and don't touch them. Stay nearby, wait, and let it take the time it needs. Try not to get angry or take their behaviour personally. What's happening is caused by an overloaded brain, not anger directed at you as a person.

- Be open to infodumping. Let the autist elaborate in depth about their special interest. When you are no longer interested, just say so.

- Listen actively and try to remember what's being said.

- Read on the lines, not between them. Practise distinguishing between reality (what was said) and imagination (what you think the autist meant but didn't say).

- If you are an educator working with autistic children: Rebel where you can. If you feel restricted by the policies and goals adapted to neurotypical children, ignore them. Don't bother with school bureaucrats. Most likely, you know what teaching method works best in practice. Do that. No one will notice.

- If you are at a party or in some other rowdy environment with an autist who is starting to feel overwhelmed, help them get away.

- Never, ever, use a screen without headphones in public.

If you are a neurotypical who wants to become better at getting along with autists, practise understanding that there are people who communicate without ulterior motives. Pay attention to the feelings of irritation and being unjustly attacked that well up in you when corrected by an autist. Then try not to react with outrage or passive-aggressive bitterness. Try laughing, for instance. Or saying thank you for teaching you something you didn't already know. It's not so bad if someone tells you it's 'especially', not 'exspecially', and that Pluto is no longer considered a planet. You can take it.

Practise getting to know your insecurities and tendency to feel wronged. When you are corrected by an autist, it's not because they want to be the one who is always right. It's because of a general sense that we need to *get things right*. And why is that important? To make life manageable and, above all, consistent.

It has nothing to do with being rude or thinking we are special.

Love and saying the opposite of what you mean

Being in a romantic relationship with a neurotypical isn't always easy. Some autists prefer to date other autists, but, of course, that's no guarantee the relationship will work. You might understand each other well, but you might also be annoyed by personality traits that too closely resemble your own.

In romantic relationships, NTs can become even more neurotypical than usual. It's as if their peculiarities are amplified. Their demands for you to be able to read their mind and understand them as they say the opposite of what they mean become even stricter, with more hidden messages, subtexts, lies, and half-truths. Being in a relationship with a neurotypical can be challenging, to say the least. But it is possible.

Often, they have a great need for physical intimacy and emotional validation. They may struggle to grasp that they are loved unless you constantly tell them so. If you want the relationship to work, you'll have to repeat yourself quite a bit.

Some neurotypicals have an enormous need for validation. It's like a leaky bucket — no matter how much water you pour into it, it always runs dry. Their need can be almost impossible to meet. If, at the same time, they are very social and feel jealous of the autist's special interests and need for alone time, it can be difficult to make the relationship work.

If you don't have such a great need for emotional validation yourself, you may fail to identify the neurotypical's. They struggle to be clear and tell you what they need, without digressions and circumlocutions. They might think you should be able to 'tell' how they feel and 'should know' when they are sad. 'Don't worry about me' may mean the opposite — '*do* worry about me'. They expect you to be considerate and fulfil their needs precisely because they tell you not to.

You should never trust a neurotypical who says they 'don't need' a birthday or Christmas present. They usually mean the opposite, so get them something anyway. Why they insist on doing this and can't just say

that a nice present would make them happy is a mystery.

Neurotypicals may have a big need to 'snuggle'. They like to sit close together on the sofa, spoon after sex, give and receive back rubs, and stroke your forearm with a gentle touch. Sometimes, it's as if they want to treat you like some kind of cuddly toy. They may feel hurt if you don't want to be as close for as long as they do. It's important to make them understand that it doesn't mean you don't love them. Sometimes they get it, sometimes not.

For autists who are hypersensitive to sensory stimuli, touch needs to be calibrated to feel good. A gentle touch can tickle and feel uncomfortable, while a firm touch often works better. Of course, you'll need to explain this to your neurotypical.

Autists have many ways of expressing love that neurotypicals aren't always used to. You simply have to teach them.

Learn to recognise your autist's love language:

Infodumping. We tell you everything about our special interest as it brings us great joy and we want to share that joy with you. If you aren't receptive in the moment, just let us know.

Alone together. We tend to enjoy parallel play. We want to be in the same room with you even if we are doing different things. One of us might be on the computer while the other is reading a book.

Social demands can be overwhelming for us, but we express our love by wanting you close and sharing a common space.

Gifts. Because we remember details, many of us are good at giving gifts that suit your personality and interests. If you have ever mentioned that you like honey, smooth chestnuts, big earrings, or the *Dragon Age* series, we'll remember it.

Stimming together. We like to regulate and balance our emotions through stimming, which involves making repetitive movements, smelling, touching, singing, or making sounds. These are things we can do together.

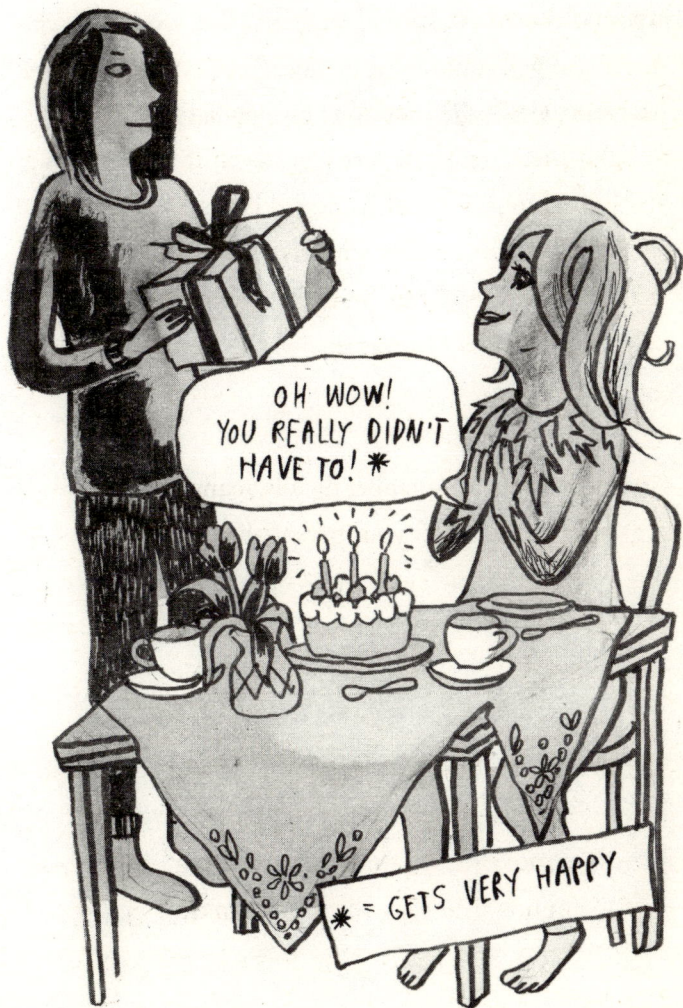

Help and support. To us, actions trump words. We are solution-oriented and will help you when you need it. We might launch a whole host of practical solutions to your problem before realising that all you wanted was sympathy and emotional support. But we are fiercely loyal and will stand by your side. Accustomed as we are to facing challenges, we don't give up easily.

Autistic voices

Henrik met his girlfriend in upper secondary school. She is autistic too, and the beginning of their relationship was quite unique.

'I fell for her instantly, hard. She liked me as a friend, but nothing more. She'd never been in love. She'd heard how you're supposed to feel but had never experienced it herself. Then there was a moment when we talked about what love is. What it means to love someone. I said, it's when you want to be around that person all the time. And that's when she realised she loves me, she said. But she never *fell in love* — instead, we went straight from friends to being a couple. You don't have to be totally obsessed with the other person in the beginning.'

Henrik has dated neurotypical people but finds it easier to be with someone who is autistic.

'We get each other and our respective difficulties.

We're both very bad at cleaning up after ourselves and doing the dishes, so our home tends to be a mess. I understand how she feels when she doesn't have the energy to tackle these things. Many couples might bicker and fight about it, but I get it. And she's just as understanding of my quirks and how I function. Right now, her special interest is Harry Potter fanfiction; she can talk about it for hours. And I'm all ears.'

Fabian: 'I wasn't happy with my schooling. But in my first year of upper secondary school, I met my girlfriend. She lit up my life.

'I saw her, and I knew she was genuine. She walked up to me with this little box of sweets, and I was like ... "Wow, thank you!" It was an origami box she'd made in her art and design class that same day. From there, we started talking about our shared interests — anime, films, and dogs. There was a film she wanted to watch, and I said I had it at home.

'"If you want, we can watch it at my place," I suggested. I said "if you want"; it's not like I forced her. So she took the bus to my place. We only ended up watching half the film, as her dad was coming to pick her up.

'When I got to bed that night, I couldn't sleep, and

the next day I wasn't even hungry. I knew what I was feeling.

'Apart from my girlfriend, I wasn't very happy with my years in school. Sometimes I think I would start over if I had the chance. But then I would never have met my girlfriend. It's a paradox.'

Paula: 'I'll tell you about this one relationship I had. We fought a lot, and half the time I didn't even know why my partner was angry. Once, I was going on a trip [from Sweden] to New York and asked if he wanted me to get him something. He said no, he didn't want anything. So, all I got him was a fridge magnet I found at the airport on my way back. He was so sulky and disappointed when I got home. Meanwhile, I'd bought lots of stuff for myself. I still don't understand how you can be upset about a thing like that.

'The same thing happened at Christmas, when he said, "I don't know what I want." So, I got him a shredder since he always refused to throw away letters without first tearing them into tiny pieces. I thought I was pretty clever. But nope, another flop. I got perfect gifts, though, because I'd told him exactly what I wanted.'

Sara: 'I worked at a hostel for a while when I was

21. Many of the guests were quite chatty, and I liked listening to people's life stories. Sometimes, after work, the staff would hang out with the guests — grab a coffee or a beer and show them around Stockholm. There was this one tourist who sought me out and suggested we meet up after my shift. Another staff member heard the way he talked, and smirked and raised their eyebrows at me, but I didn't get it. The tourist asked if I knew of any parties we could go to. I didn't. But I could always cook us a Swedish dinner. So, after my shift we went to my place. Once there, I realised he wanted us to kiss. "But I have a boyfriend," I said. He got very upset; apparently, I should've mentioned it earlier.'

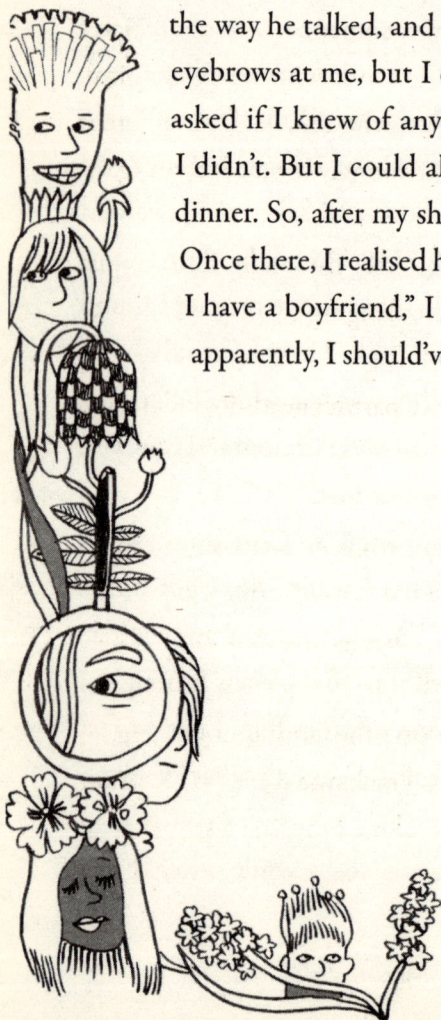

TIPS: LOVE

Try to find a caring type, someone who appreciates your strengths. Things *can* work with a neurotypical, but it needs to be someone who understands different ways of functioning or is genuinely open to learning.

It's your choice. Don't settle for being chosen just because you find dating challenging.

Most importantly, your NT partner needs to understand the following:

- Struggling to start and finish certain things is not the same as laziness.
- Sensory overload is not being 'dramatic' or 'oversensitive'.
- Avoiding eye contact isn't the same as not caring.
- Having a meltdown isn't making a scene for attention.
- Needing recovery and alone time isn't a sign that you love them any less.

Be open about your needs from the beginning. If you move in with a neurotypical partner, you probably won't be able to pull as much weight as they do, so you'll need to be with someone who accepts working more or doing a little more around the home than you. All the while, you'll compensate with interesting facts from your spot at the computer and take care of the aspects of cohabitation that require a stubborn autist. Explain that you won't change with time and autism cannot be overcome by willpower. It's important to make your partner understand that you don't love them any less just because you sometimes need to withdraw or don't want physical contact.

Autists are experts at unintentional flirting. More than once, I have happened to meet a neurotypical who shares my special interests and been so happy that I wanted to talk to them nonstop. I'm just as surprised every time I realise that my enthusiastic conversing has been received as flirting. So, if you are an unintentional flirt, remember: some neurotypicals don't understand that we are primarily interested in the topic of conversation. They might misunderstand and think you are interested in them.

Develop a healthy vigilance against people. Don't believe everything new acquaintances tell you; don't assume they are telling the truth. Unfortunately, autists are duped, exploited, and sexually abused more often than most. Dishonest people choose their victims carefully and have an incredible ability to sniff out autists since we struggle to spot lies and make for easy prey.

People lie heedlessly, especially when shielded by online anonymity. Remember that there are different degrees of friendship; some are just acquaintances. Only trust people you know well.

Learning

'Can you see the forest over there?' 'No, the trees are in the way.'

This is an old joke that plays on different ways of acquiring knowledge. Often, autists don't see the forest for the trees, while the neurotypical sees the forest first and only later discovers it's made up of trees.

When **Henrik**, who is autistic, started university after upper secondary school, he made a habit of filming his lectures. If he only heard them once, it was too much information for him to process, no matter how many notes he took. He got bogged down in the details and couldn't keep up. But if he recorded each lecture, he could watch it at home in peace and quiet.

Henrik studied part-time for a master's degree in engineering. But his time at university could be challenging. During lectures, he couldn't listen and take notes at the same time. Help with notetaking from other students didn't work, as he couldn't understand their thought process. What helped him the most were recordings.

'So, I got a camera and started recording the lectures, with the lecturers' approval. That way, I could pause and rewind as I watched.

'I'm very good at taking in a lot of information, condensed. But there's a limit. In two hours, I can absorb three times as much as a neurotypical. But then that's it; I can't process more. Everyone else took longer, but they got everything. While I struggled like crazy and still could only absorb a certain portion of the course materials. After a while, my brain just stopped working. Then I couldn't study the next day either.'

As an autist, you often need to do what Henrik did and find your own ways of learning, since the educational system is adapted to a neurotypical approach. At most universities, you can get an individual education plan, which means you study at a slower pace than others. But this might not be the right path for you. Thanks to our ability to laser-focus, many autists can process a lot of information in a short space of time. We can be far ahead of other students, finding the needle before we even notice the haystack. You'll need to find what works for you to get through the educational path of your choosing.

When Henrik started working, he discovered that his way of learning was a much better fit in the workplace.

'At work, I need to process a lot of information in a short time, and that's where my capacity lies. I can absorb a crazy amount, grasp it quickly, and even get it down on paper. There, I can play to my strengths. It takes others much longer.'

The educational system today looks different than it did when I went to school in the 1980s and '90s. A lot has changed when it comes to pedagogy and the way we view knowledge, and teachers use new teaching methods. I'll try to explain.

When I was in school, it was more autism friendly. You could cram for a test without needing to answer questions about *how* you arrived at the correct answer. Knowing the information was enough. Because of this, I did well in school and got good grades. But now, when my eight-year-old daughter is doing her reading

comprehension homework, it's not enough for her to correctly identify what the text is about. She must also be able to specify whether the correct answer is found 'on the lines, between the lines, or beyond the lines'. We struggled for a long time with that piece of homework. Not even I — a grown, university-educated author — understood what she was being asked to do. But today's schoolchildren are expected to handle a high level of abstraction and critically analyse themselves.

Back in my day, it was quiet in the classroom, and oral presentations weren't so important. Even though it could at times get rowdy, the baseline for learning was that it should be silent — not that several parallel group projects should be going on at once. If you were shy, and struggled to perform socially, you could still get good grades.

In summary, today's teaching methods are a poor fit for autistic students. They probably aren't great for any student, beyond a few mature, confident, and extroverted group types — but for an autist, they are especially counterproductive. Unfortunately, school is something you'll have to find your own strategies to cope with. It gets better later on in life, I promise.

TIPS: LEARNING

As a student, you have the right to receive support and additional adjustments. In Sweden, this right is enshrined in the Education Act. If you are studying at university, you can apply to get a tutor, help with notetaking, and extensions for your assignments and exams. You can also apply to the Swedish Board of Student Finance to study part-time but with full financial aid. Vocational schools usually have specially trained educators. Each country is different, though, so make sure you know what resources are available to you.

If it's not working out, and you aren't getting the adjustments you need despite your best efforts, change schools. When the only option is to continue a fruitless struggle with a negative impact on everyone involved, it's better to move on. This may sound drastic, but convincing school staff who lack knowledge about autism can be very difficult.

For parents and guardians: Be prepared to take personal

responsibility for some of your child's education. Practise social situations and role-playing, assist with homework, always be present. Try to understand your child's behaviour as a response to something. Cut back your working hours if you can afford it. Don't waste too much time battling over adjustments; instead, change schools if you aren't met with understanding — while also accepting that the situation may never be entirely satisfactory. Our educational system is designed for neurotypical children, and in some countries, like Sweden, home-schooling isn't allowed, creating a very difficult situation for many autistic children. In the worst case, school becomes something your child must simply endure, with your help. In the best case, you'll encounter knowledgeable and dedicated staff.

Carefully consider which professions _wouldn't_ be a good fit before applying to university or for a job. For autists, this tends to include jobs that involve high levels of stress and noise, meeting lots of new people, and significant unpredictability. Don't bother with such industries. Find a profession where you can draw on your strengths. It needs to be a safe place where you will be accepted for who you are. The ideal situation is to make a living from your special interests, but that can be challenging. Finding the right place and the right circumstances will take time and require significant effort. Remember that it's illegal for employers to discriminate based on your disability.

Don't put too much hope in government support. Your life is here and now and shouldn't be spent in call queues. You have so much more to offer the world. Untangle yourself from the web of government bureaucracy if you are caught in it. Make your own adjustments with the help of friends and family. It's easier said than done if you don't have understanding relatives, but strive to help yourself as much as possible.

Don't trust the welfare system to take care of you. Social structures and the job market were created by neurotypicals for neurotypicals. Instead, invest your energy in finding your own niche.

It's expensive to be autistic. More than your neurotypical friends you'll need a financial cushion, since you might not be able to work as much as they do. As with everything else in society, there is — of course — a class issue here. It's easier to carve out your own life and be independent if you have money.

Fears

Besides death, neurotypicals have two major fears: losing control and being humiliated. More than the supernatural, ghosts, and zombies, they fear other people. Most of all, perhaps, they fear themselves. At its core, this fear is about their dread of being ostracised from the group and becoming lonely. For many, that's the worst scenario imaginable.

You often see this in horror films. Even if the films are populated by monsters on the surface, another terror lurks beneath: the fear of human madness.

Many horror stories culminate in the revelation that the real threat came from within, from the subconscious. In a common plot twist, the protagonist has imagined it all and is, in fact, suffering from delusions. The monster existed only in the protagonist's mind.

But is that really so frightening? Well, not for someone who — like the autist — is used to living in a reality where sensory stimuli strike you with their full force, other people express themselves and react incomprehensibly, and your own experiences are questioned and misinterpreted.

Horror stories are fuelled by a somewhat exaggerated fear of mental illness. To an autist, at least, mental instability isn't as frightening as the thought that ghosts really do exist, like remnants of evil human deeds living on long after they were committed. But the origin of this fear comes from the neurotypical's deep-seated terror of being excluded from the group.

What about autists? We fear not knowing what will happen: What's next, what's going on, what's the mood in the room right now, how will they react, what will they say? Will I be able to manage? Is there an escape route? There is no knowing what's coming around the bend.

If you live with the uncertainty and confusion that a different way of functioning entails, it can feel as though anything might happen next. You are constantly bracing to have your view of reality overturned or for someone to object to what you say; expecting to be misunderstood, to misinterpret, or to be overwhelmed by sounds, light, smells, or tastes. This is the fear we try to overcome by creating routines and rituals, and doing things the same way each time. This is why we don't want things to change, at least not when we find ourselves in a neurotypical setting.

I don't want to go so far as to suggest that we live inside a perpetual horror film, but I think most autists have a rather undramatic relationship to the dark corners of their subconscious. If, for instance, you experience musical notes as being different colours (this is called synaesthesia and is more common in autists), perhaps a waking dream or delusion isn't the scariest thing you can imagine. Going a little mad — what's there to be afraid of?

Casimir: 'They can be so scared of things that are icky. I swear, I don't think my classmates have ever emptied a wastebasket. They have this weird idea that they'll get sick. They think they'll get super ill and die if a bird poops on them.'

The hunt for safe zones

So, is it possible for neurotypicals to change and practise becoming more autistic? Can they learn to mask their peculiarities to give us a break? Yes, they can. The problem is that they often lack the incentive because there are so many of them that they don't need to. Neurotypicals who do understand autism almost always have an autist in the family.

In some respects, society was more autism-friendly in the past. It was slower, contained fewer stimuli, and didn't impose the same demands for flexibility, constant change, and social competence. Why has this shifted? It's because of political decisions and technological developments. Digitisation and automation mean that people are now expected to handle things on their own that they previously received help with from others.

With screens entering our lives, public spaces became much louder, and it's harder to shield yourself from the noise. But recently, there has been a backlash. More and more people object to others talking in spaces that used to be quiet, such as libraries.

And yet, very few companies have begun to consider autists and other hypersensitive individuals as potential target groups.

In Brazilian cities such as São Paulo and Rio de Janeiro, autists have access to priority seating on buses and the metro. Alongside symbols for pregnant women, wheelchair users, and the elderly are autism stickers. This has been the case since the late 2010s, when the law was changed to include autists among those with special needs in public spaces. The reasons cited included accessibility, inclusivity, physical integrity, and the citizen's right to public services. Decision-makers wanted to help autists move about more freely and thereby strengthen their independence. In certain shops, autistic individuals also have priority in the checkout line.

In the United States and Canada, retailers such as Target and Sobeys have introduced special hours that are 'sensory-friendly' — when lights are dimmed, the number of customers limited, and the music over the speakers is muted. In the US and Brazil, there are amusement parks specifically catering to families with autistic children. There are also autism-friendly cruises.

An app that aids autists on public transport has been piloted in Australia. It offers tips for managing sensory overload and guides its users to alternative, quieter routes.

In Sweden, we haven't gotten quite as far. The other year, the government-owned passenger train operator, SJ, abolished 'quiet compartments' on its trains since passengers didn't respect the rule and talked out loud anyway. Instead, they introduced the option 'second-class calm' — a carriage where conversations are allowed. But they should be subdued, explains press officer Tobbe Lundell in the local paper *Göteborgs-Posten*: 'If you're talking, you should have to lean in to hear what the other person is saying.'

Stockholm has initiated a project called 'Guide to Silence', providing tips on the city's quiet places. And when international pop sensation Zara Larsson said in a TikTok video that people should be allowed to talk in the cinema, she faced harsh criticism. Most people wanted to keep the silence in the cinema, as one of the few spaces where it still exists.

However, some neurotypicals in this debate had a hard time understanding why others' talking bothers those who want silence. They couldn't relate to sensory hypersensitivity and the need to be fully absorbed in the film — couldn't grasp that there are those who can't block out competing sounds and miss out on the film if others are talking.

Instead, they interpreted the advocates of silence as 'elitists' and accused them of harbouring 'contempt' towards their fellow humans, and of having other nasty traits. Oddly enough, those who advocate for silence and consideration towards others can be perceived as a kind of oppressor.

A few times a year, though, all neurotypicals become a little more autistic. It happens around the holidays. Suddenly, everything must be done exactly the same way as before, according to a strict routine. Nothing can change. The food has to be the same as during last year's Eid celebration; for Christmas, the same woollen gnomes must be hung in the same places around the home, and the same TV programs must be watched at the same time. The same music as last year should be played, and the same guests invited. Often, even the conversations and the comments are the same, as though they were scripted.

If you are a practising Jew, for instance, the candles must be lit from a certain end of the Hanukkah menorah, and you must hold the cup with which you wash in your left hand, not your right. During Shabbat, you must only rest and read, not switch on or off any lamps, not use the stove or oven, not carry keys, press buttons, ride elevators, bike, ride horses, or use electronics.

During holidays, neurotypicals put aside their usual demands for renewal. Following rules correctly becomes the main thing. Everything should be done the same way as last time. Nothing must change.

On the other hand, you could view the very obligation to celebrate holidays as quintessentially neurotypical. A few times a year, every NT must do the same thing simultaneously to show that they belong to the same community.

Casimir is in lower secondary school and was diagnosed with autism when he was four years old. He doesn't like when it's crowded and there are lots of people around him. When he rides the bus or goes to the cinema or theatre, he doesn't want to sit next to someone he doesn't know. Casimir attends a music school and plays the organ. By the time he was twelve years old, he could play the same repertoire piece that applicants to the Stockholm Royal College of Music's master's degree must audition with.

On weekends, he practises the organ four hours a day. After school on weekdays, he manages about an hour. At the moment, he almost exclusively plays Bach. His favourite piece used to be 'Fantasia and Fugue in G Minor', but now he has played it so much he has grown a bit tired of it.

When Casimir listens to music, he sees patterns and colours. He also hears all the different parts, which is practical when playing the organ.

'I can't describe it, but I imagine it's roughly what your thoughts are like if you're born blind. If so, all you have is your sense of hearing and touch. I don't see colours when I play different notes myself. All that comes into my mind is a feeling that's associated. I can't describe it. I think about other things when I play. I zone out, it happens automatically.'

At Casimir's school, there are many students with neurodevelopmental conditions.

'It's a unique environment,' says Casimir's mother, **Åsa**. 'There are so many students with neurodevelopmental conditions that much of the school is adapted to them; they're the baseline. Their instruments are their special interests, and those who are skilled at their instrument gain status and are elevated.'

Neurotypical behaviours considered 'normal'

- Lacking special interests and being interested in a little bit of everything on a general level.

- Taking many breaks and quickly switching between different tasks when working on an important project that requires focus.

- Facing new situations without preparing for what's to come.

- Never making definitive plans and 'keeping things open' until the last moment.

- Rearranging schedules on short notice.

- Answering complex questions immediately without first thinking about what to say.

- Skimming information before making big decisions.

- Not questioning rules and authority but blindly obeying the will of the group.

- Not intervening when someone is treated unfairly because they 'don't want to get involved'.

- Saying the opposite of what they mean without irony.

- Ingratiating themselves with someone before speaking ill of them behind their back.

The road to peace of mind

Living in the neurotypical world is hard. If you try to suppress your autism and compete on their terms, I'm afraid you will lose. It may sound harsh, but it's the truth.

Living as an autist in a neurotypical society, you need to learn to distinguish between what's important and what's unimportant. The neurotypical world may try to convince you that everything is equally important to endure, but that's not the case.

For autists, the most crucial thing is to learn to conserve your energy. The easiest way to do this is to scale back. Simplify your life. Do less and say no. Work *with* your autism instead of against it. Lower your stress levels. Build a predictable existence.

In summary, I can tell you that sleep, love, protecting your own wellbeing, and finding the right occupation are important. A varied diet, having lots of friends, cleaning, and strict hygiene are not.

If you feel anxious or depressed, under no circumstances should you self-medicate. If you need therapy and have the opportunity, spend time finding a really good therapist. Don't settle for the first one you see, nor for some therapy app.

It's not certain that therapy will help, however. It depends on how it's designed. I would say it's essential to choose a therapist who knows autism, even if you are seeking help for issues like depression or anxiety. A psychologist who doesn't know autism won't understand you, and you'll run the risk of being misinterpreted or receiving treatment that doesn't suit you.

Some psychologists struggle with treating clients with autism. They aren't willing to accept that autism has biological causes and neither results from childhood trauma nor is curable through therapy. Some tend to trivialise and dismiss autism diagnoses, and that won't help you. You can't base therapy on the idea that there is no fundamental difference between autists and neurotypicals.

Nor will you be helped by therapy that aims to make you appear more neurotypical by masking your autism. On the contrary, this can be devastating. It's like subjecting gay people to conversion therapy or prohibiting transgender individuals from correcting their gender. You deserve to be yourself. Moderate, strategic adaptation is enough. It's a matter of learning when and how much you need to adapt — or not. Try to find a neurotypical you trust who can help you when needed.

Masking is not the path to peace of mind. True peace arises within you and cannot be measured by someone else. Everything you have to offer the world is already in the depths of your soul. It has nothing to do with how many superficial social tricks you learn.

Here is a statement that may seem discouraging: it doesn't get easier. It doesn't matter how skilled you become at playing the neurotypical game — if you train until you win first prize in social competence and agility. It doesn't stop being difficult just because you know how to do it.

You might learn to put on a convincing smile, but the pretence will still feel like slowly scraping a fork against a porcelain plate. How do I know? Because I have practised for 47 years, and it doesn't get easier with time — if anything, it gets harder. We autists need to be allowed to be ourselves.

Therefore, my advice is to find your self-esteem

by being *more* autistic, not less. Don't run away from yourself by trying to be something you are not. You aren't someone to be 'cured' or a failed human specimen to be improved. Your top priority should be your own mental health, and the list of true musts is much shorter than you think.

Other things that are good for your wellbeing:

If you can't manage to exercise — walk! Walking alleviates anxiety.

Find your temple. A religious one if you believe in God, or some other place of peace and quiet that you can go to.

Invest in a good pair of noise-cancelling headphones, earplugs, and comfortable sunglasses.

Keep stimming. Embrace your autistic traits.

Forgive the neurotypicals. Most of them are doing their best. They don't know much about autism, and it takes time to learn if you lack the experience. Autism is complicated.

Quiz: How neurotypical are you?

1. If the person you are talking to doesn't look you in the eyes, you feel:

1. Annoyed and excluded. What a rude person!
2. Puzzled. Why aren't they meeting my gaze?
3. Unfazed. I listen actively to what they are saying and don't think about eye contact.

2. You and a friend are meeting up for some pizza. Five minutes before you are set to meet, your friend sends you a text, suggesting a different restaurant. How do you react?

1. Good idea, I'm happy to change plans. Wasn't really in the mood for pizza anyway.
2. It doesn't matter — I don't care what we eat. The

most important thing is that we get to see each
other.

3. I feel overwhelmed, and my whole body screams:
   NO. We had agreed on pizza! Now I have to reset.
   How do I even find this other place?

**3. Your friend shows you their new trousers and asks
what you think. 'Be honest!' they say. The trousers
aren't attractive. What do you reply?**

1. They look great! Keep them.
2. They're not my style, but you look good in them.
3. If I'm honest, they don't fit you well, and I don't
   like the colour.

**4. In a meeting at school, your teacher asks the
students for their opinions on the atmosphere in
class. You think several things are working poorly.
What do you do?**

1. I think to myself that it's probably strategically
   smarter to save my criticism for another time, since
   my teacher won't appreciate me airing it in front of
   everyone. I say that everything is great, and I have
   no objections.

2. I sit silently, as I don't want to get involved and risk displeasing my teacher ahead of grading. Just because they say they welcome criticism, it doesn't mean it will be well received.

3. My brain overflows with ideas for improvements. To avoid forgetting them, I quickly blurt out everything I'm thinking, accidentally interrupting a classmate in the process, and forgetting to raise my hand and waiting my turn. In my eagerness to cover all proposed solutions without taking up too much space, I speak quickly and concisely.

5. Your favourite body lotion or deodorant is being discontinued. What do you do?

1. I don't have a particular favourite; I switch between brands and like trying new products. Some variety is nice.

2. I think it's a shame, since the product worked well, but simply order an equivalent instead and don't think more about it.

3. I search through shops up and down the country for remaining products, involve my loved ones in the hunt, email the manufacturer, and beg for the product to come back. I scour the internet and

cry with joy when I find a German online retailer charging a small fortune in shipping, order all remaining products, and will never open the last bottle because then it's really gone.

6. What's the first thing you do when you have bought a new piece of clothing?

1. Try it on and study myself in the mirror, checking if it fits well and looks as good as in the picture on the website. I take a selfie and send it to a friend to ask what they think.
2. Put the item away in my closet while I contemplate whether to keep it.
3. Try it on to feel the material against my skin. Then I cut off all the tags that itch and chafe.

7. You are writing an essay with a friend who emails you a bibliography they have compiled. It's spelled correctly and free of errors. How do you react?

1. Feel relieved that they took care of the boring part, so I don't have to.
2. Copy the list into the essay without reading it too carefully.

3. Shiver with delight at how perfectly constructed the list is.

8. While on a walk, you notice a bush, an advertisement, and a jacket in the same exact shade of green. How do you react?

1. Huh? Why would I walk around noticing the colour of things?
2. Don't think about it until a friend points it out. But it's nice, I guess?
3. With delight! I love seeing patterns and details around me that fit together perfectly.

9. You are on the bus, and the passengers next to you slurp, chew, and sniffle loudly. How do you react?

1. I don't notice because I'm busy speaking loudly over FaceTime to a friend, without earphones.
2. I feel uncomfortable and change seats during the journey to try to escape the sounds.
3. I wear earplugs and ear defenders, so luckily I don't hear any of this. Besides, I travel standing up, as I don't like sitting next to people I don't know.

10. How often do you clean?

1. I clean occasionally, doing a blitz with the vacuum when needed. I'm neither meticulous nor sloppy.
2. I like it sparkling clean and organised around me. I hate dirt and often think about how to remove invisible bacteria.
3. Clean? Sometimes when someone is coming into my room, I pick up dust bunnies with my hands and throw them in the trash.

Mostly ones:

You couldn't be more neurotypical if you tried. You love chitchatting with your hairdresser and feel energised from having lots of brief social interactions with new people. When someone sends you a text message, you prefer to call them back; it's too time-consuming and inefficient to write back and forth. You don't have a particular hobby but like joining other people's — it's fun to do things in a group. You have a hard time around people who don't get your jokes and can't keep up with you.

Mostly twos:

You have many neurotypical traits and are an introverted and sensitive person. You are open and find it easy to empathise with others' feelings.

Mostly threes:

You probably already have an autism diagnosis. If not, immediately seek out the nearest neurodevelopmental screening unit.

SOURCES OF INSPIRATION AND FACTS

How to Handle Neurotypicals: a field survival guide for the neurodivergent by Abel Abelson (2020)

The Asperkid's Secret Book of Social Rules by Jennifer Cook (2022)

A Field Guide to Earthlings: an autistic/Asperger view of neurotypical behavior by Ian Ford (now Star Ford) (2010)

Nonverbal Communication by Albert Mehrabian (2007)

Why Johnny Doesn't Flap: NT is ok! by Clay & Gail Morton (2015)

Unmasking Autism by Devon Price (2022)

Autismhandboken ('The Autism Handbook') by
   Katarina A. Sörngård (2018)

Allism Spectrum Disorders: a parody by Terra Vance
   <psychcentral.com/blog/aspie/2018/09/
   allism-spectrum-disorders-a-parody#Allism>

'Neurotypicals: listen to our words, not our tone' from
   the blog *Autistic Science Person*
'In Autism Study, It's All About the Eyes', *Yale
   Medicine Magazine* <medicine.yale.edu/
   news/yale-medicine-magazine/article/
   in-autism-study-its-all-about-the-eyes/>